KEN FULLER'S
FUN AND DANCES

Ken Fuller and Margaret Horrocks being presented with the first NASD
'Pennine Trophy' by the manager of the Locarno Ballroom in 1962

First published 1996
by
T. A. Whitworth,
42 Newbold Back Lane, Chesterfield,
Derbyshire, S40 4HQ.

Reprinted 1998

ISBN   0-9501927-5-9

British Library Cataloguing in Publication Data:

Fuller, Ken

Fun and Party Dances

I. Title   II. Whitworth, T. A.

793.33

ISBN 0-9501927-5-9

FOREWORD

We are very pleased indeed to write the foreword to this book of party dances since we hold Ken Fuller in high regard. He is a quiet, unassuming person with an excellent knowledge of dancing and his sequence dances have brought pleasure to people all over the world. His services to sequence dancing have been recognised by the recent award of the Certificate of Merit issued by the 'Dancing World' magazine. We wish him many more years of good health knowing that he will gain immense satisfaction when he looks back over his dancing life and realizes the happiness he has brought to others.

JOHN AND JEAN LEGGE *(Huddersfield)*

The following (with others) wish to be associated with these remarks:-
Jim Howes and Rose (Hyde); Harold and Emmy Hammond (Stockport); Tim and Dorothy Edmunds (Denton); Morris and Joan Sheard (Huddersfield).

AUTHOR'S ACKNOWLEDGEMENTS

I would like to express my sincere thanks to the following:-

To *Mrs. Susan Baker* for type-setting the manuscript and advising on the layout.

To *David Charlesworth* for designing the front cover and frontispiece. (David is one of Derbyshire's best-known professional artists and designers.)

To Pat Price for help with the cartoon on the front page.

To *Alan Whitworth* for advice and encouragement and the preparation of the book for publication. I can recommend to anyone his 'Modern Sequence Dancing For All' (1994) and 'History of Sequence Dancing and Script List' (1995).

To my present dance partner *Mrs. Alwyn Raffo*. She has done sterling work in helping to promote the cause of sequence dancing in our region.

KEN FULLER *(July 1996)*

iii

KEN FULLER

Ken Fuller has been active in sequence dancing since 1952 - it can be said to have been his life's work. In this time he has arranged more than 300 sequence dances of high quality. His Red Rose Tango and Kingston Quickstep were thought to be of sufficient merit to be included in the first handbook of modern sequence dances produced by the Official Board of Ballroom Dancing in May 1966. Although he has won more than a dozen awards in inventive sequence dance competitions, prize-winning has never been his main motivation. Like Bill Botham, he arranged many dances "just for fun, sometimes my own, sometimes for other people's". He is much concerned with good technique in dancing and is meticulous in preparing his scripts - nevertheless, for him, sequence dancing is a pastime to be enjoyed and this book contains some of his zany humour.

Ken Fuller is noted for his helpfulness, tact and persistence - he has always been willing to put his shoulder to the wheel and help people where he could. He was secretary of the Manchester MC's Club from 1956 to its closure in 1996. He arranged all the annual dances and was editor of its 'Focus' journal in its later years. Like most MC's his work has been largely unseen and unsung - his rewards are to be found in the hearts of his many friends.

Ken with Alwyn Raffo, his present partner

CONTENTS

INTRODUCTION

Novelty or fun dances are designed to put life into the proceedings on festive occasions - to get people to laugh and shout and mix together. Many of them have their own music and some have imitative actions of hands, arms and body. In general they are easy to learn so that all can take part whatever their level of dancing skill.

The dances in this book have been arranged by Ken Fuller over more than 30 years - many are popular in the north. The first group are line and circle dances which are ideal for dancers without a permanent partner. American Line Dancing has become very popular in the UK in recent times and most of these dances can be performed in this style. Some line dances have been demonstrated at recent sequence dancing festivals.

The second section consists of partner dances and details are provided to make most of them progressive - what Alex Moore has described as 'mixer dances'.

Dances in the last chapter have a Scottish flavour and can be danced to the lively foot-tapping music found in the recordings of Jimmie Shand. In modern sequence there are relatively few dances in the 6/8 marching rhythm which tends to lift the heart.

Northern Dance Services *(18 Commercial Street, Shipley, West Yorkshire, BD18 3SP - Tel.:- 01274 586829)* supply a list of scripts of more that 160 party dances.

Books which include some of the older and more traditional party dances, such as the Palais Glide, Lambeth Walk, Farmer's Wife and Hokey Cokey, are:-

Party Dances, Nancy Clarke, IDTA   *(reprinted 1993)*

Party Dances and Games, ISTD   *(reprinted 1993)*

CHAPTER 1

Line and Circle Dances

THE STING-BEAT

The Sting theme tune ('The Entertainer') or a slow jive.
Time 4/4. Tempo 31/32.
Danced in lines, no hold, man's and lady's steps the same.
Commence facing LOD, arms relaxed, elbows bent.

Bar Count

Bar	Count	
1	QQS	LF fwd slightly DC; almost close RF to LF; LF fwd slightly DC.
2	QQS	RF fwd slightly DW; almost close LF to RF; RF fwd slightly DW (face LOD on bars 1 and 2).
3	QQQQ	LF fwd down LOD, turn slightly L; tap RF at side of LF, face DC; correcting turn - RF fwd down LOD, turn slightly R; tap LF at side of RF, face DW.
4	QQS	Correcting turn - LF fwd down LOD; tap RF at side of LF; repeat tap (tap firmly as a stamp).
5-8	---	Repeat pattern of bars 1-4 commencing RF, end facing LOD.
9	QQS	LF fwd down LOD; cross RF behind LF; LF fwd down LOD leaving RF in place and swivel to R to face against LOD, end weight on LF.
10	QQS	RF fwd against LOD; cross LF behind RF; RF fwd against LOD.
11	SS	Point LF fwd against LOD; point LF rearward down LOD.
12	QQS	Point LF fwd against LOD inclining body backwards; point LF rearward down LOD inclining body forward; close LF to RF with weight correcting body inclination, face against LOD.
13-16	---	Repeat pattern of bars 9-12 commencing RF against LOD, end facing LOD in commencing position.

1

NON-PROGRESSIVE STING BEAT

If non-progression is preferred bars 1-8 may be replaced by the following 8 bars:-

1	QQS	LF to side towards centre; almost close RF to LF; LF to side towards centre with RF moving towards LF.
2	QQS	RF to side towards wall; almost close RF to LF; RF to side towards wall with LF moving towards RF.
3	QQQQ	LF to side towards centre; tap RF at side of LF; RF to side towards wall; tap LF at side of RF.
4	QQS	LF to side towards centre; tap RF at side of LF; repeat tap (stamps).
5-8	---	Repeat pattern of bars 1-4 commencing RF to side towards wall.
9-16	---	Follow on as previous page.

Why was Ken Fuller born in Salford?
Because he wanted to be "near his mother".

What did the red-haired, strict-tempo dance teacher say to his wife when his beard caught fire?
Flo, Flo, Quick Quick, Blow!

Why did the one-handed dance teacher cross the road?
To get to the second-hand shop!

Why did the 'Come Dancing' viewer dust his television screen?
Because he thought he saw a tellymark!

Why was the skeleton crying?
Because he had nobody to dance with!

What dance do sequence dancing ducks like the best?
The quackstep!

THE RAGMATAZZ

Tempo 44. Ragtime music: 'Maple Leaf Rag', 'Rags and Tatters', etc.
Danced in lines of 6 or more depending on size of room.
Both man and lady dance same steps throughout. No hold.
Commence facing LOD. No turn during the dance.

Bar	Count	
1	SS	LF fwd down LOD; RF fwd down LOD, only short steps keeping feet flat using a bouncy movement, arms swinging, elbows bent.
2	SS	Repeat bar 1.
3	SS	LF to side and slightly fwd; swing RF across LF and point to floor (slight stamp).
4	SS	RF to side and slightly fwd; swing LF across RF and point to floor (slight stamp).
5	SS	LF back against LOD thrusting R shoulder fwd, a deliberate movement; close RF back to LF correcting shoulder line.
6	SS	Repeat bar 5.
7-8	SSSS	Repeat bars 3 and 4.
9	SS	LF to side to centre; close RF to LF.
10	SS	LF to side to centre; close RF to LF without weight (tap).
11	SS	RF to side towards wall; close LF to RF.
12	SS	RF to side towards wall; close LF to RF without weight (tap).
13	SS	LF fwd down LOD; close RF to LF.
14	QQS	Thrust knees fwd (Q); straighten legs (Q); repeat first movement but count 'S'.
15	SS	Repeat bar 5, very short steps.
16	QQS	Repeat bar 14.

Dance in a bouncy manner with knees relaxed.

> *The late James Wilson of Glasgow had printed on his cards:- "I need your feet to run my dance."*

3

SING-ALONG STROLL

Time 4/4. Tempo 28/30 (may also be danced to 6/8 rhythm).
Man's and lady's steps the same throughout.
Commence facing LOD, inside hands are joined throughout the dance.
The full width of the hall may be used for the lines.
Use Barn Dance medleys and the good old songs to sing to.

Bar	Count	CHASSÉ L AND R WITH LOW AERIALS - ZIG-ZAG TO R - CHECK AND TWINKLE
1	QQS	All LF to side towards centre; close RF to LF; LF to side towards centre swinging RF fwd and across LF to low aerial.
2	QQS	RF to side towards wall; close LF to RF; RF to side towards wall swinging LF fwd and across RF to low aerial.
3	QQQQ	Extend LF fwd and across RF, slight turn L; RF to side towards wall; LF back under body, slight turn R; RF to side towards wall, face LOD, medium steps.
4	SQQ	LF fwd and across RF, relaxing knee (check); transfer weight back to RF; LF to side, very short step, face LOD.

ZIG-ZAG TO L - CHECK AND TWINKLE - SWAYS TO L AND R

5	QQQQ	RF fwd and across LF, slight turn R; LF to side towards centre; RF back under body, slight turn L; LF to side towards centre, face LOD, medium steps.
6	SQQ	RF fwd and across LF, relaxing knee (check); transfer weight back to LF; RF to side, very short step, face LOD.
7	SS	LF to side towards centre, sway to L, relaxing knees; transfer weight to RF, relaxing knees, face LOD, sway R.
8	SS	Transfer weight to LF, sway L, relaxing knees; transfer weight to RF, sway R, relaxing knees, face LOD.

4

FWD WALKS - REARWARD WALKS AND AERIALS - SQUARE

9	SS	LF fwd down LOD; RF fwd relaxing knee (check).
10	SS	LF back against LOD raising RF to low fwd aerial, headlines to R; RF back against LOD raising LF to low fwd aerial, headlines to L.
11	SQQ	LF fwd down LOD; RF to side towards wall; close LF to RF, face LOD.
12	SQQ	RF back against LOD; LF to side towards centre; close RF to LF, face LOD.

SWAY CHASSÉS TO L AND R - FWD AND REARWARD TWINKLES - TAKE A BOW

13	SQQ	LF to side towards centre swaying L, relaxing knee; transfer weight to RF; close LF to RF, face LOD.
14	SQQ	RF to side towards wall swaying R, relaxing knee; transfer weight to LF; close RF to LF, face LOD.
15	QQQQ	LF fwd down LOD; close RF to LF; LF back against LOD; close RF to LF.
16	SS	With feet in place bend fwd from the waist in a bowing movement, arms moving rearward; straighten body to normal position raising joined hands above head (S). Lower hands to normal height to commence next sequence (S).

He thought he was Lord of the Dance
But really, he hadn't a chance,
His technique was paltry,
His footwork was faultry.
He was given one point for his 'prance'.

He really was bad in the rumba
But tried to impress this cute number.
His face turned bright red
When she left him and said,
"You're as green as a garden cucumber."

FESTIVAL PARADE

Time 4/4. Tempo 30/32. Music: Any Barn Dance medley.
Commence all facing LOD, inside hands joined, 6 or 8 in a line. All
dance on same foot throughout.

Bar Count

1	SS	With inside hands joined, all fwd along LOD on LF crossing slightly over RF; fwd RF crossing slightly over LF.
2	SS	Repeat bar 1.
3	QQQQ	Fwd LF along LOD; point (tap) RF fwd; fwd RF; point LF fwd.
4	SS	Balance fwd on LF with RF closing without weight; balance rearward on RF with LF closing without weight.
5	QQS	Fwd LF, RF, LF along LOD releasing hold and turning to R on last step to face against LOD and then clap hands.
6	QQS	Fwd RF against LOD; fwd LF turning to L; side RF against LOD facing wall with LF brushing to RF. Dancers are now in line, one behind the other, all facing wall closing up slightly to dancer in front. Place hands on hips or waist of the dancer in front as for the Conga.
7	SS	Side LF along LOD swaying to L relaxing knees as RF closes to LF without weight; side RF against LOD swaying to R relaxing knees as LF closes to RF without weight.
8	SS	Repeat bar 7.
9	QQQQ	Move fwd towards wall LF, RF, LF, point or slide RF rearward as in the Conga with the leading dancer commencing to curve to L to face centre.
10	QQQQ	Repeat Conga movement on opposite feet RF, LF, RF, LF, the leading dancers will now be moving towards centre with the rear dancers still curving round.
11	QQQQ	Dance 2 more bars of Conga movement to finish
12	QQQQ	all facing centre, one dancer behind the other in lines. Release hold.

13	QQS	LF to side against LOD; cross RF loosely over LF; LF to side against LOD turning R to face LOD and then clap hands.
14	QQS	RF fwd along LOD; LF fwd; close RF to LF.
15	QQQQ	Slap hands on thighs; clap hands at waist height; place hands on shoulders; clap hands at shoulder height.
16	QQQQ	Point L thumb over L shoulder, relaxing knees and turning head to L; straighten knees correcting headline; point R thumb over R shoulder, relaxing knees and turning head to R; straighten knees correcting headline and join inside hands to repeat sequence.

This may be performed as a circle dance. In a large hall an inner circle may be formed but must dance independently of the outer circle.

Hints on Dancing by Professor Dan Shoo

Professor Dan Shoo is an authority on dancing although on taking his tests on steps he fell down them.. Dan has brought out many books on dancing - he is a regular attender at the local library. He is the inventor of that popular movement the '39 Steps'.

1. *A strong lead is necessary for the lady but give her a comfortable collar to go with it.*

2. *Always use Cherry Blossom for a polished performance.*

3. *Keep on the 'beat' as much as possible if your local police officer does not object.*

4. *A good twinkle could make you into a star.*

5. *Don't overdo a rock turn or you may feel yourself nodding off.*

6. *Only move one foot at a time as moving both feet together gives a bad shoulder line - however, it does put you a jump in front of the other dancers.*

SAMBA CIRCLE and LINE SAMBA

Time 4/4. Tempo 54/56.
All join hands in a circle, all commence on LF, same steps throughout.
Lady on the right but others may join in without a partner.
Dance freely and in a lighthearted manner.

The Line Samba is the same dance in lines across the full width of the hall.

Bar	Count	THREE WALKS AND POINT - REARWARD TWINKLE - STEP, POINT
1	1.2	All LF fwd towards centre of circle; RF fwd.
2	1.2	LF fwd towards centre of circle; point RF fwd, short step.
3	1.2	RF back; close LF to RF.
4	1.2	RF fwd towards centre of circle; point LF fwd, short step.

		REARWARD WALKS TO COMMENCING POSITION - KNEES BEND TO L AND R
5	1.2	LF back, swinging R shoulder fwd; RF back swinging L shoulder fwd.
6	1.2	LF back swinging R shoulder fwd; close RF back to LF, inside hands still joined. Now back in commencing position.
7	1.2	With slight foot turn to L, bend knees; straighten knees correcting turn.
8	1.2	With slight foot turn to R, bend knees; straighten knees correcting turn.

		STEP, SWING TO L - STEP, SWING TO R - REPEAT STEP, SWINGS
9	1.2	LF to side, short step; swing RF fwd and across LF to low aerial.
10	1.2	RF to side, short step; swing LF fwd and across RF to low aerial.
11	1.2	Repeat bar 9, step and swing.
12	1.2	Repeat bar 10, step and swing.

FORWARD AND REARWARD TWINKLES - KNEE SLAPS - CLAP OWN HANDS

13	1.2	LF fwd towards centre of circle; close RF to LF.
14	1.2	LF back to place; close RF back to LF leaning fwd from waist, knees relaxed. Release hands.
15	1&2	Slap knees (or just above knees) 3 times to the time of 1&2 (L hand to L knee, R hand to R knee).
16	1&2	Straighten body and clap own hands 3 times to the time of 1&2, shoulder height.

Rejoin inside hands for next sequence.

THE PARTY LINE

A line dance, but may be danced in a circle, if preferred.
Time 4/4. Tempo 33/34. Music: Barn Dance medleys, jives.
Commence on LF, no hold, face LOD.
Man's and lady's steps the same throughout.
Arms tucked in loosely, elbows bent.

Bar	Count	JIVE CHASSÉS L AND R - CLOSE, KICKS - REARWARD AND FWD TWINKLES - HEEL 'STAMPS'
1	Q&Q	LF to side; half close RF to LF; LF to side, small steps;
	Q&Q	RF to side to wall; half close LF to RF; side RF, small steps.
2	QQQQ	Close LF to RF; swing (kick) RF fwd to low aerial; close RF bk to LF; swing (kick) LF fwd to low aerial.
3	QQQQ	LF back against LOD; close RF to LF; LF fwd; close RF to LF.
4	QQS	With feet together in place, sharply raise heels then lower to floor with a slight 'stamp', a deliberate movement (Q); repeat the heel movement (Q); repeat one more time (S).
		Move arms up and down slightly in time with the heel movements, emphasising the downward heel movements.
		Shout "1-2-3" in time to the movements.
5-8		Repeat exactly bars 1-4.

THE PARTY LINE (continued)

STEP, TAPS FWD - REARWARD WALKS AND AERIALS - REARWARD AND FWD TWINKLES - SWAYS AND CLAPS

9   QQQQ   LF fwd down LOD, slight body turn L; tap RF at side of LF slightly apart; RF fwd down LOD, slight turn R; tap LF to RF slightly apart.

10   SS   LF back raising RF fwd to low aerial (S); RF back raising LF fwd to low aerial.

11   QQQQ   LF back against LOD; close RF to LF; LF fwd; close RF to LF.

12   QQQQ   The feet remain in place during this bar. Sway to L from waist and clap hands twice at L shoulder level (QQ); sway to R from waist, clap hands twice at R shoulder level (QQ), face LOD.

SIDE WALKS TO L - LF AND RF TAPS - SIDE WALKS TO R - RF AND LF TAPS

13   QQS   Straightening body and turning to face DC, LF to side moving towards centre; RF fwd and slightly across LF; LF to side towards centre turning R to face LOD with RF brushing towards LF.

14   QQQQ   RF to side towards wall; tap toe of LF to floor behind R heel; LF to side towards centre; tap toe of RF to floor behind L heel.

15   QQS   Turning to face DW, RF to side towards wall; LF fwd and slightly across RF; RF to side towards wall turning L to face LOD with LF brushing towards RF.

16   QQQQ   LF to side towards centre; tap toe of RF to floor behind L heel; RF to side towards wall, face LOD; tap toe of LF to floor behind R heel.

Music is the soul (and heel) of dancing.
Your feet were made for dance shoes.
Since going metric my left foot is. now a left metre.

SOCIAL TWO STEP

Time 2/4 or 6/8. Tempo 52.
All commence facing LOD, inside hands joined about shoulder height.
May be danced in 2's (lady and man), 3's (a lady on either side of a
man) or in lines for any number across the full width of the hall.
Man's and lady's steps are same throughout; both start with the LF.
A good tune is 'Scotland the Brave'.

Bar	Count	
1	1.2	LF fwd down LOD; RF fwd down LOD.
2	1.2	LF fwd down LOD; RF fwd down LOD and commence turning to R to end backing LOD, rejoin inside hands.
3	1.2	LF back down LOD; RF back down LOD.
4	1.2	LF back down LOD; close RF to LF facing against LOD.
5-8	---	Repeat bars 1-4 still commencing on LF. Finish facing LOD as commencing position.
9	1.2	Side LF to centre; close RF to LF.
10	1&2	Side LF to centre; stamp RF twice at side of LF (&2, the first stamp rather sharply).
11	1.2	RF to side towards wall; close LF to RF.
12	1&2	Side RF to wall; stamp LF twice at side of RF (&2, the first stamp rather sharply).
13	1&2	Pas de Basque to L towards centre, LRL.
14	1&2	Pas de Basque to R towards wall, RLR.
15	1.2	LF to side towards centre (short step with a slight stamp); swing RF diag across LF to low aerial.
16	1.2	RF to side towards wall (short step with a slight stamp); swing LF diag across RF to low aerial.

Although varying slightly from the original script the above version is
the one danced in many areas.

The Social Two Step is rather energetic and is not suitable for
dockers, chess players or politicians.

THE BLACKPOOL SWING

Time 4/4. Tempo around 44. Music: 'Blackpool Belle'.
Commence all partners facing LOD, inside hands joined, all on same foot, same steps throughout the dance. Dance lightheartedly.
The full width of the hall may be used or, if preferred, dance in lines of 8, 10 or 12, etc.

Bar	Count	OPEN CHASSÉS - WALKS - CHECK AND REARWARD SWAY - OPEN CHASSÉS - SOLO REVERSE TURN
1	QQS	All LF fwd along LOD slightly DC; part close RF to LF; extend LF slightly DC.
2	QQS	RF fwd along LOD slightly DW; part close LF to RF; extend RF slightly DW.
3	SS	LF fwd along LOD; RF fwd along LOD.
4	SS	LF fwd along LOD relaxing knee, checking step, RF in place; sway rearward on RF.
5	QQS	Repeat bar 1, open chassé, LRL.
6	QQS	Repeat bar 2, open chassé, RLR.
7	SS	LF fwd along LOD, toe pointing DC commencing to turn L (lady same way); RF to side along LOD still turning L. Release hold on first step.
8	SS	LF back under body along LOD; close RF to LF all now facing against LOD, rejoining inside hands, still in lines.
9-16	---	Repeat movement of bars 1-8 commencing against LOD to end facing along LOD.

		SIDE, CLOSE - SIDE, SWING TOWARDS CENTRE - SIDE, CLOSE - SIDE SWING TOWARDS WALL
17	SS	LF to side towards centre; close RF to LF, face LOD.
18	SS	LF to side towards centre; swing RF diag across LF.
19	SS	RF to side towards wall; close LF to RF, face LOD.
20	SS	RF to side towards wall; swing LF diag across RF leaving still crossed.

12

LF CHECK AND CHASSÉ TOWARDS CENTRE - RF CHECK AND CHASSÉ TOWARDS WALL

21 SS   LF fwd diag to wall, relaxing knee, checking step, RF in place; transfer weight back to RF.

22 QQS LF to side towards centre; close RF to LF; LF to side towards centre, face LOD.

23 SS   RF fwd across LF diag to centre relaxing knee, checking step, LF in place; transfer weight to LF, face LOD.

24 QQS RF to side towards wall; close RF to LF; RF to side towards wall closing LF to RF without weight, face LOD.

FWD WALKS AND TAP - REARWARD WALKS AND TAP - SIDE SWINGS

25 SS   LF fwd along LOD, inside hands still joined; RF fwd along LOD.

26 SS   LF fwd along LOD; point (tap) RF fwd along LOD, short step (check).

27 SS   RF back against LOD; LF back against LOD.

28 SS   RF back against LOD; close LF back to RF with a tap. Release hold.

Dance last 4 bars in a jaunty, swingy manner.

29 SS   LF to side towards centre; swing RF diag across LF (clap and swing same time each bar).

30 SS   RF to side twds wall; swing LF diag fwd across RF.

31 SS   LF to side twds centre; swing RF diag fwd across LF.

32 SS   RF to side towards wall; close LF to RF without weight and clap own hands, face LOD.

Clap own hands on swings in bars 29-31.

MELODY FOXTROT (side by side)

Partners join inside hands, facing down LOD and dance on the 'same foot'. The hold is released on turning, rejoining hands as soon as possible.
If dancing as a line dance limit the lines to 6 to negotiate the corners.

13

THE CRACKA-JACKA

Time 4/4. Tempo 34 (or to taste).
Commence in lines, all facing LOD.
Man and lady on same foot throughout. No hold until bar 12.
Body movements may be freely expressed.
Music: Any sequence jive, e.g. 'Java Jive'.

Bar	Count	**3 SIDE WALKS TO L - 3 SIDE WALKS TO R - SWAYS - CHASSÉ TO L**
1	QQS	Side LF to centre, elbows bent, very slight turn L; cross RF loosely over LF moving towards centre but facing DC; LF to side, slight turn R to face LOD.
2	QQS	Repeat movement of bar 1, commencing RF and moving towards wall, slight turn L at end to face LOD, feet apart.
3	QQQQ	Sway L, slight relaxation of both knees; sway R; sway L; sway R.
4	QQS	Extend LF to side towards centre: RF half closes towards LF; LF to side towards centre, RF in place ending feet apart.
5-8	---	Repeat movement of bars 1-4 commencing on RF moving first towards wall, bar 8 will be chassé to R towards wall ending feet apart.

		L AND R ARM FLINGS - CLAPS AND ELBOW JERKS - L AND R ARM FLINGS
9	QQQQ	Fling L arm above head moving leftwards away from head, palm fwd (Q); lower hand to shoulder height bending from elbow leaving elbow in place (Q); repeat raising and lowering of L arm (QQ).
10	QQQQ	Repeat movement of bar 9 but using R arm.
11	QQQQ	Clap both hands at chest height (Q); jerk elbows back to sides (Q); repeat clap and elbow jerk (QQ).
12	QQQQ	Fling L arm above head moving leftwards away from head, palm fwd (Q); lower hand to shoulder height bending from elbow leaving elbow in place (Q); repeat using the R arm.

14

CHASSÉ L AND TAP - CHASSÉ R AND TAP - LF AND RF TAPS - SWINGS

13 QQQQ All join inside hands where possible. LF to side to centre; half close RF to LF; LF to side to centre making slight body turn R; tap RF near to LF facing DW, hands still joined.

14 QQQQ Side RF to wall turning slightly to face LOD; half close LF to RF; RF to side to wall making slight body turn L; tap LF near to RF facing DC.

15 QQQQ LF to side to centre, body turn R; tap RF near to LF, face DW; RF to side to wall making slight body turn L; tap LF near to RF facing DC.

16 QQQQ LF to side to centre, face LOD; swing RF across LF to low aerial; side RF to wall; swing LF across RF to low aerial. Release hold to commence next sequence.

If dissatisfied with your partner try the jive throwaway - if you make it strong enough you might not see her again!

SOCIAL STROLL

Time 4/4. Tempo around 32.
Man and lady on 'same foot' throughout.
*All commence on LF facing along LOD, **arms linked** (do not overcrowd the lines).*

Bar Count WALKS ALONG LOD - SIDE SWAYS AND CLOSES

1 SS All LF fwd along LOD; RF fwd along LOD.

2 SS LF fwd along LOD; close RF to LF.

Dance bars 1 and 2 in a jaunty manner.

3 SQQ LF to side to centre swaying L; RF to side to wall; close LF to RF.

4 SQQ RF to side towards wall swaying to R, LF to side to centre; close RF to LF.

All still facing along LOD with arms linked.

SOCIAL STROLL (continued)

WALKS ALONG LOD - SOLO FOUR STEP - SWINGS AND CLOSES

5   SS   LF fwd along LOD; RF fwd along LOD unlinking arms and placing at sides.

6   QQQQ LF fwd towards DC turning to L, no hold; RF to side and back; LF back along LOD, all now side by side facing against LOD; close RF to LF - dancers again linking arms as at start, facing against LOD.

7   SQQ   Side LF to centre swinging RF slightly across LF; side RF, small step; close LF to RF.

8   SQQ   Side RF to wall swinging LF slightly across RF; side LF, small step; close RF to LF all facing against.

WALKS AGAINST LOD - SIDE SWAYS AND CLOSES

9   SS   All fwd LF against LOD; RF fwd against LOD.

10 SS   LF fwd against LOD; close RF to LF.

Dance bars 9 and 10 in a jaunty manner.

11 SQQ   Side LF to centre swaying to L; RF to side, small step; close LF to RF.

12 SQQ   Side RF towards wall swaying to R; LF to side; RF closes to LF.

WALKS AGAINST LOD - SOLO FOUR STEP - L AND R SWAYS

13 SS   LF fwd against LOD; RF fwd against LOD unlinking arms and placing at sides.

14 QQQQ All LF fwd slightly DC against LOD turning to L, no hold; RF to side and back; LF back against LOD, all now facing LOD, side by side; close RF to LF - dancers again linking arms as at start.

15 SS   LF to side to centre swaying to L, RF in place; sway to R on RF.

16 SS   LF to side to centre swaying to L, RF in place; sway to R on RF and brush LF to RF.

All face LOD as at start, commencing hold.

THE CAROLINER

Time 4/4. Tempo 32/34. Commence in lines facing LOD. Lady's
steps same as man's throughout.
Barn Dance or Palais Glide medleys, preferably vocal.

Bar	Count	FWD AND BACK TWINKLES - KNEE BENDS TO L AND R - JIVE CHASSÉS
1	QQQQ	All LF fwd down LOD, inside hands joined; close RF to LF; LF back against LOD; close RF to LF.
2	QQQQ	With feet together make slight turn to L bending knees, face DC; straighten knees; repeat knees bend still facing DC; straighten knees turning to face LOD. When turning feet lift toes slightly off floor swivelling on heels.
3	QQQQ	With feet together make slight turn to R bending knees, face DW; straighten knees; repeat knees bend still facing DW; straighten knees turning to face LOD, hands still joined.
4	Q&Q Q&Q	LF to side towards wall; RF half closes to LF; LF to side; repeat chassé to R towards opposite wall. Short steps in the chassés, RF, LF, RF.
5-8	---	Repeat bars 1-4, hands still joined.

		STEP, TAP FWD AND REPEAT - TURNING FOUR STEP - SIDE SWINGS TO L AND R
9	QQQQ	LF fwd down LOD, slight body turn L; tap (point) RF fwd down LOD; RF fwd down LOD, slight body turn R; tap (point) LF fwd down LOD, only short steps.
10	QQQQ	LF fwd down LOD commencing to turn L, hands released; RF to side still turning; LF back against LOD; close RF to LF rejoining inside hands. Face against LOD.
11	QQQQ	LF to side towards wall, short step; swing RF diag across LF turning heads to L; side RF towards opposite wall; swing LF across RF turning heads to R.
12	QQQQ	Repeat bar 11, side swing to L and R, inside hands still joined.

STEP, TAP FWD AGAINST LOD AND REPEAT - TURNING FOUR STEP - THIGH SLAPS - HAND CLAPS - HANDS UP

13-14	---	Repeat bars 9 and 10 moving against LOD, end facing LOD but do not rejoin hands.
15	QQQQ	Bending fwd, slap front of thighs, i.e. LH to L thigh, RH to R thigh; repeat slaps; straightening body, clap hands at shoulder height; repeat hand clap.
16	QQS	Bending fwd slap thighs once; clap hands once at shoulder level, straightening body; raise arms above head for count of 'S'. Rejoin inside hands to commence sequence, face LOD.

THE SKYLINER

Time 4/4.   Tempo 30/32.   Music: 'Beautiful Sunday', 'Jingle Bell Rock', 'Sugar, Sugar' or similar jive-type recordings.
Commence facing LOD, danced in lines, man and lady 'same foot' throughout.   No hold except bars 7 and 8 (optional).   Lines may use the full width of the hall.

Bar Count

1	Q&Q	All dancers LF to side to centre; half close RF
	Q&Q	towards LF; LF to side, all short steps; repeat jive chassé to R towards wall. RLR.
2	QQQQ	LF to side to centre; swing RF across LF to low aerial; RF to side to wall; swing LF across front of RF to low aerial (the swings are diag fwd and danced with slight kick action).
3	QQQQ	LF to side to centre; almost close RF to LF; LF to side to centre; raise R knee off floor, knee bent, slapping R knee with palm of R hand.
4	QQQQ	Repeat movement of bar 3, chassé and knee slap, commencing on RF, moving to R towards wall and slapping L knee with L hand.
-6	---	Repeat bars 1, 2, jive chassés and side swings.
7	QQQQ	LF fwd down LOD; RF fwd; LF fwd down LOD; swing RF fwd to low aerial.
8	QQQQ	RF back against LOD; LF back; RF back against LOD; close LF to RF without weight.

Inside hands may be joined during bars 7 and 8 (optional).

9	QQQQ	Point LF to side towards centre; close LF to RF without weight; repeat point and close.
10	SS	Side LF to centre, wide step, relaxing knee; drag RF to LF closing without weight.
-12	---	Repeat movements of bars 9 and 10, points and drag, commencing on RF and moving towards wall.
13	QQQQ	LF fwd down LOD, slight body turn L; point (tap) RF fwd slightly in front of LF; RF fwd down LOD, slight body turn R; point LF fwd slightly in front of RF.
14	QQQQ	LF back against LOD; point RF at side, feet almost closed; RF back against LOD; close LF to RF with weight.
15	QQQQ	Bending knees slightly and bending fwd from waist, slap front of thighs with hands (i.e. palm of L hand slapping L thigh and palm of R hand slapping R thigh at same time) (Q); repeat thigh slaps (Q); straightening body clap hands together at chest height (Q); rpt hand clap (Q).
16	QQS	Raise R arm slightly and slap under elbow with palm of L hand (Q); raise L arm slightly and slap under elbow with palm of R hand (Q); raise arms above head keeping them apart (S).

Lower hands to start next sequence, arm and body movements may be freely expressed.

He attempted a double reverse spin.
What a mess he found himself in.
All hands were on deck,
His feet round his neck,
So they gave him a tonic and gin.

(Sorry, I couldn't get gin and tonic to rhyme)

Professor Dan Shoo says that the performance of the double reverse spin is improved considerably by putting grease under each sole (making sure that none gets on the heels).

THE CIRCLE CONGA

Time 4/4. Tempo 33.
Dancers form a circle, one behind the other with hands on the waist of person in front, left sides towards centre of circle as in the ordinary Conga. All dance same steps commencing on LF.

Bar	Count	
1	1.2	All LF fwd circling anti-clockwise; RF fwd; LF fwd;
2	3.4	slip RF to side and slightly back without weight, head turns to R.
3	1.2	RF fwd still circling anti-clockwise; LF fwd; RF fwd;
4	3.4	slip LF to side and slightly back without weight, head turns to L.
5	1.2	LF to side towards centre of circle releasing hold
6	3.4	commencing to turn inwards to L; RF fwd and across turning to face centre (hub) of circle; LF fwd towards centre of circle; tap or point RF slightly fwd, short step clapping own hands at same time.
7	1.2	RF back twds own places joining inside hands in circle;
8	3.4	LF back; RF back to original places; point or tap LF at side of RF, short step.
9	1.2	LF to side circling clockwise; close RF to LF.
10	3.4	LF to side circling clockwise; swing RF across LF with a kicking action.
11	1.2	RF to side mvg anti-clockwise; close LF to RF.
12	3.4	RF to side circling anti-clockwise; swing LF across RF with a kicking action.
13	1.2	LF fwd towards centre of circle releasing hold; RF fwd making ¼ turn to R.
14	3.4	LF to side towards centre of circle leaving RF in place; swing hips to L, slight body turn to L, fairly sharp movement.

| 15 | 1.2 | RF to side towards own place; LF fwd and across; |
| 16 | 3.4 | RF to side, dancers now one behind the other leaving LF in place; swing hips to R, slight body turn R, fairly sharp movement. |

Emphasise every fourth step.

HARRY-LIME FOXTROT

May be danced as a Conga in single file with Conga hold.
All dancers will dance on the same foot of course but this should not cause any problems to the ladies.

PARTY CIRCLE

Time 4/4. Tempo 30.
Danced in a circle, inside hands joined bars 1-12, then Shadow Hold.
Danced on 'same foot' throughout.
Commence on LF, lady on man's R.
Music: Barn Dance medleys or good old songs to sing to.

Bar	**Count**	**FWD SQUARE - L & R SWAYS - CHASSÉ TO L**
1	SQQ	All LF fwd towards centre of circle; RF to side; LF closes to RF.
2	SQQ	RF back; LF to side; RF closes to LF in original places.
3	SS	LF to side swaying L; sway to R, LF almost closing without weight.
4	QQS	LF to side; close RF to LF; LF to side, RF almost closing without weight.
		REARWARD SQUARE - R AND L SWAYS - CHASSÉ TO R
5	SQQ	RF back away from centre of circle; LF to side; RF closes to LF.
6	SQQ	LF fwd towards centre of circle; RF to side; LF closes to RF.
7	SS	RF to side swaying R; sway to L, RF almost closing without weight.
8	QQS	RF to side; LF closes to RF; RF to side, LF almost closing without weight.

21

PARTY CIRCLE (continued)

ZIG-ZAG TO R - CHECK AND TURN - ZIG-ZAG TO L - CHECK AND TURN

9   QQQQ   LF fwd slightly across RF, turning slightly L; RF to side; LF back under body turning slightly R; RF to side.
All move anti-clockwise on zig-zag.

10   SQQ   LF fwd slightly across RF relaxing knee (check); replace weight to RF turning slightly L; LF to side, small step, all face towards centre of circle.

11   QQQQ   RF fwd slightly across LF, turning slightly R; LF to side; RF back under body turning slightly L; LF to side.
All move clockwise on zig-zag.

12   SQQ   RF fwd slightly across LF relaxing knee (check); replace weight to LF turning slightly R; RF to side all face towards centre of circle, small step. All release hands.

FWD WALKS - REARWARD WALKS - L AND R SWAYS - LADY'S SIDE, CLOSES

13   SS   Taking Shadow Hold with lady on man'ns R side, both LF fwd towards centre of circle; RF fwd relaxing knee (check).

14   SS   LF back away from centre of circle; RF back and slightly rightwards (man only) with LF closing back to RF without weight. Lady is now almost in front of man, both facing inwards, lady has her back to man.

15   SS   LF to side swaying to L in loose Shadow Hold; sway to R on RF with LF closing without weight, and then release hold.

16   QQQQ   Man remains in place during this bar, lady side LF; close RF to LF; LF to side and slightly back; RF closes to LF, lady now on L side of previous partner. Join inside hands to recommence the sequence.

Dancing adds pleasure to leisure in no small measure.

22

CHAPTER 2

Partner Progressive Dances

PASO ESPAÑA

Time 2/4. Tempo 58. Music: 'Y Viva España'.
Man's steps. Lady normal opposite unless stated. Commence with partners facing LOD with inside hands joined in Open Hold.

Bar	Count	
1	1.2	LF fwd along LOD; RF fwd along LOD.
2	1.2	LF fwd along LOD; close LF to RF.
3	1.2	Mark time with LF on spot; mark time on spot with RF.
4	1.2	Mark time on spot with LF and RF, still in Open Hold.
5	1.2	LF fwd along LOD; RF fwd along LOD commencing to turn inwards, to R (lady to L).
6	1.2	LF to side along LOD now facing wall and partner releasing hold with R hand and taking lady's R hand in own L hand; still turning slightly RF back, slightly under body in loose contra whisk position placing R hand at back, palm outward about waist high (lady may take hold of gown hem with L hand). Check. End facing DW against LOD, lady facing DC against LOD.
7	1.2	Man remains on spot, feet in place, lady starts
8	1.2	to circle clockwise round man, RF, LF, RF, LF to end facing DW still circling R, clasped hands raised as lady commences to move behind man.
9	1.2 .	Man remains on spot, feet in place as lady continues to
10	1.2	circle round man, RF, LF, RF, LF to end facing DC against LOD having made a full circle round man in 8 steps. Lower clasped hands to normal height in Contra Open Hold.
11	1.2	LF fwd and across against LOD with slight stamp turning to L (lady to R); close RF to LF facing wall and partner taking Double Hold.

PASO ESPAÑA (continued)

12   1.2   Mark time on spot, LF, RF.

13   1.2   LF back towards centre (lady RF back towards wall) pushing lady away in throwaway movement releasing hold; RF back towards centre holding R arm across body almost chest high, L arm across back of body almost waist high (no arm movements for lady).

14   1.2   LF back towards centre (lady RF back towards wall); close RF near to LF arm positions still as bar 13.

15   1.2   LF fwd towards wall and partner (lady RF fwd); RF fwd arms still as bar 13.

16   1.2   LF fwd towards wall and partner turning sharply L to face LOD (lady turns R) joining inside hands; close RF to LF now in commencing position.

To make progressive: Man veers to L in bars 15 and 16 to next partner in front, lady veering L to next partner behind, or man use bars 1 and 2 for with lady progressing.

Smile when you dance and make it progressive.

To have the correct orientation is a step in the right direction! Modern sequence dancers often choose their own orientations! This is recognised in Professor Dan Shoo's definition:-

> *"Modern Sequence Dancing is an art form in which all dancers do the **same** steps at the **same** time but in **different** directions."*

A conceited dancer boasted that he had dancing in his blood. His teacher said, "You must have poor circulation, it's not reached your feet yet!"

MACNAMARA'S TWO STEP

Time 6/8. Tempo 48. Music: 'Macnamara's Band'.
Man's steps. Lady normal opposite. Commence with partners facing
LOD with inside hands joined in Open Hold.

Bar	Count	
1	1&2	Fwd LF down LOD, move RF slightly towards LF, extend LF fwd.
2	1&2	Fwd RF down LOD, move LF slightly towards RF, extend RF fwd.
3	1.2	Fwd LF down LOD, fwd RF.
4	1.2	Point LF fwd, point LF slightly to side parallel with RF.
5	1&2	Pas de Basque to L - to centre LRL.
6	1&2	Pas de Basque to R - to wall RLR.
7	1.2	Side LF to centre releasing hold (lady side RF to wall), close RF to LF.
8	1.2	Side LF turning to R to face wall and partner, close RF to LF.
9	1.2	Fwd LF to wall and partner, fwd RF.
10	1.2	Fwd LF, close RF to LF.

Bars 9 and 10 may be danced in a jaunty manner.

11	1.2	Clasp lady's R hand in own R hand (1), clasp lady's L hand in own L hand above clasped R hands (2). Hands are clasped just above waist height.
12	1.2	Release R hands and reclasp above clasped L hands (1), release L hands and reclasp above clasped R hands (2).
13	1.2	Release both hands and stamp or tap LF to side twice bending knee, feet about six inches apart. Clap twice in time with the LF, hands level with L shoulder.
14	1.2 ·	Repeat bar 13.
15	1&2	Adopt waltz hold and with body turn to R
16	1&2	dance 2 bars natural waltz turn with gent pas de valse on last bar to finish in commencing hold and position.

To make progressive: In bars 9 and 10 both man and lady veer slightly L to next partner.

KLAXON SWING

Time 4/4. Tempo 34. Music: 'Clap Clap Sound'.
Partners facing LOD, inside hands joined in Open Hold.
Man's steps given. Lady normal opposite unless otherwise stated.

Bar	Count	WALKS - HOP - POINT CLOSES - CHASSÉS TO R AND L WITH SWINGS
1	QQQQ	LF fwd along LOD, inside hands joined; RF fwd along LOD; LF fwd along LOD; hop on LF raising RF slightly off the floor, knee bent.
2	QQQQ	Point RF to side towards wall and partner (lady points LF towards centre and partner); close RF to LF without weight; point RF to side towards wall; close RF to LF without weight. Only short steps on the points.
3	QQQQ	RF to side towards wall (lady LF to side towards centre) releasing hold, partners preparing to change places with lady crossing in front of man; close LF to RF; RF to side towards wall (lady LF to side towards centre); swing LF diag across RF to low aerial at the same time clap hands at chest height. Partners now in opposite places. Face LOD.
4	QQQQ	LF to side towards centre (lady RF to side towards wall) preparing to change places with lady again crossing in front of man; close RF to LF; LF to side towards centre (lady RF to side towards wall); swing RF diag across LF to low aerial at the same time clap hands at chest height. Partners now in original places, face LOD and rejoin inside hands.

WALKS - HOP - POINT CLOSES - BACKWARD AND FORWARD TWINKLES - SCOOP

5	QQQQ	RF fwd along LOD, inside hands joined; LF fwd along LOD; RF fwd along LOD; hop on RF raising LF slightly off the floor, knee bent.

6	QQQQ	Point LF to side towards centre (lady point RF towards wall); close LF to RF without weight; point LF to side towards centre; close LF to RF without weight. Only short steps on the points.
7	QQQQ	LF back against LOD with slight inward turn to R (lady slight inward turn to L on RF); close RF to LF facing DW (lady faces DC) taking double hold in PP; LF to side along LOD; close RF to LF still double hold.
8	SS	LF to side along LOD, a wide stride relaxing knee; close RF to LF with scoop action and a gradual outward turn to face LOD, release lady's R hand. Now in commencing hold and position.

To make progressive: In bar 8 man omits the scoop and moves fwd LF, RF, LF, RF to next lady in front (QQQQ).

THE 'COKERNUT' HOP

Time 6/8. Tempo 46/48.
Music: 'I've got a lovely bunch of 'Cokernuts''.
Man's steps. Lady normal opposite. Commence with partners in Double Hold in promenade position facing down LOD.

Bar	Count	
1	1.2	Side and fwd LF along LOD in double hold, point RF fwd raising front hands and lowering rear hands, body swaying rearwards.
2	1.2	Fwd RF along LOD, point LF to side and fwd lowering front hands and raising rear hands, body swaying fwd.
3-4	---	Repeat bars 1 and 2.
5	1.2	Fwd LF slightly diag to centre releasing hold and turning to L (lady to R), side RF along LOD still tng.
6	1.2	LF back along LOD joining inside hands in contra open hold, hop on LF with R knee bent - RF crossed slightly over LF.

THE 'COKERNUT' HOP (continued)

7-8	---	Repeat movement of bars 5-6 against LOD commencing RF turning to R (lady to L). Finish facing LOD, inside hands joined.
9	1.2	Point LF to floor crossing over RF, point LF fwd and to side, LF now diag fwd to centre from RF.
10	1.2	Place heel of LF on floor - L toe raised, point toe to LF to floor on same spot - L heel raised. Release hold.
11	1.2	Twist outwards to L (lady to R) arms swinging to R, twist inwards arms swinging to L.
12.	1.2	Repeat twist as bar 11 then adopt commencing hold and position.
13	1.2	Side and fwd LF swivelling to R (inwards) to face agst LOD, close RF halfway back to LF without weight.
14	1.2	Side and fwd RF against LOD swivelling to L to face LOD, close LF halfway back to RF.
15	1.2	Side and fwd LF along LOD releasing lady's L hand (lady RF fwd commencing to turn to R under man's raised L arm), fwd RF along LOD (lady side LF still turning to R) Allemande.
16	1.2	Side and fwd LF along LOD (lady RF) taking lady's L hand in own R hand, close RF to LF in commencing hold and position.

To make progressive: Man remains on spot bars 15 and 16 while lady makes solo R turn to next partner in front.

They say that too many new dances are coming out but are always ready for them when they appear.

It's a question of keeping up with the Jones's.

I wonder, is there any chance of the Jones's giving up their sequence dancing?

BOSTON BARN DANCE

Time 4/4. Tempo 32/34. Music: Barn Dance medleys.
Commence with partners facing LOD with inside hands joined in Open
Hold. Man's steps. Lady normal opposite unless otherwise stated.

Bar	Count	WALKS AND POINT - CHANGE OF PLACES TO R AND TO L - WALKS AND POINT
1	QQQQ	LF fwd along LOD; RF fwd along LOD; LF fwd along LOD; point (or tap) RF at side of LF (parallel position).
2	QQS	RF to side to wall commencing to change places, with lady passing in front of man; close LF to RF, hold released; RF to side to wall with LF closing LF to RF without weight. Join inside hands, partners now in opposite places facing along LOD.
3	QQS	LF to side to centre commencing to move back to own places, lady again passing in front of man; close RF to LF, hold released; LF to side to centre with RF closing to LF without weight. Rejoin inside hands, partners now in commencing position facing along LOD.
4	QQQQ	RF fwd along LOD; LF fwd along LOD; RF fwd along LOD; point (or tap) LF at side of RF (parallel position).

DIAG SOLO WALKS AND CLAP OWN HANDS - FWD WALKS - L AND R SWAYS - TURNING TWINKLE

Bar	Count	
5	QQQQ	LF diag fwd towards DC releasing hold (lady moves DW); RF fwd; LF diag fwd DC and swivel inward to R to face partner and wall (lady swivel L); part close RF to LF without weight clapping own hands.
6	QQQQ	RF fwd towards wall and partner (lady LF fwd); LF fwd; RF fwd towards wall and partner; close LF to RF without weight joining both hands in Double Hold.
7	SS	LF to side along LOD, RF in place and sway to L; sway to R against LOD with LF part closing towards RF without weight.

29

BOSTON BARN DANCE (continued)

8   QQQQ   LF to side along LOD, front hands released, turning outward; close RF to LF, partners now facing along LOD; LF back against LOD; close RF to LF, partners in commencing position and hold.

To make progressive: In bar 6 man will veer slightly leftward to next partner in front, lady will veer slightly leftward also to next partner behind.

BARN DANCE BLUES

Time 4/4. Tempo 32/33. Music: Barn Dance medleys.
Man's steps. Lady counterpart unless otherwise stated.
Commence partners facing LOD, inside hands joined in Open Hold.

Bar	Count	FWD WALKS AND SWING - REARWARD WALKS - FWD WALKS - REARWARD TWINKLE AND FWD LOCK
1	QQS	LF fwd along LOD in Open Hold; RF fwd along LOD; LF fwd along LOD swinging LF fwd to low front aerial.
2	QQS	RF back against LOD; LF back against LOD; RF back against LOD (check).
3	SS	LF fwd along LOD, slight turn L; RF diag fwd along LOD, relax knee, slight sway fwd (check).
4	QQQQ	Transfer weight back to LF, slight inward turn; RF closes back to LF; LF diag fwd along LOD; RF crosses behind LF.

		FWD WALKS & SWING - REARWARD WALKS - FWD WALKS - REARWARD AND FWD SWAYS
5	QQS	LF fwd along LOD still in Open Hold; RF fwd along LOD; LF fwd along LOD swinging LF fwd to low front aerial.
6	QQS	RF back against LOD; LF back against LOD; RF back against LOD (check).
7	SS	LF fwd along LOD, slight turn L; RF diag fwd along LOD, relax knee, slight sway fwd, man face DC (lady face DW).

30

8	SS	Replace weight to LF swaying rearward; sway fwd on RF turning to face LOD and brushing LF to RF. Adopt Double Hold in PP.

PROM WALKS - CHASSÉ TO L - R AND L SWAYS - TWINKLE TO PP - STEP, POINT

9	SS	LF to side along LOD in PP; RF fwd and across along LOD turning to R (lady to L).
10	QQS	Side LF along LOD fcg wall and partner; RF closes to LF; LF to side along LOD leaving RF in place (check).
11	SS	Sway to R, LF in place; sway to L, RF in place.
12	QQQQ	Extend RF to side against LOD turning to L (lady turns to R on LF); LF closes to RF with weight, almost facing LOD; RF fwd and across along LOD; point LF fwd and to side DC (lady point towards DW) and release hands.

DIAG SOLO WALKS - WALKS TO PARTNER - SIDE CHASSÉ (LADY ALLEMANDE) - SIDE CHASSÉ

13	QQS	LF to side moving DC (lady moves DW); move RF loosely across LF; LF to side towards DC turning to R to face wall and partner and clap own hands.
14	QQS	RF fwd towards wall and partner; LF fwd; RF fwd twds partner brushing LF to RF and adopting Double Hold.
15	QQS	LF to side along LOD releasing lady's L hand as she commences to turn R under man's raised L arm); RF closes to LF (lady still turning R); LF to side along LOD facing wall and partner retaking lady's L hand in Double Hold (check).
16	QQS	RF to side against LOD, slight turn L (lady R); LF closes to RF still turning; RF back against LOD releasing lady's R hand, partners now facing LOD in commencing position and hold.

To make progressive: Man moves leftwards in bar 14 to next partner in front; lady moving leftwards to next partner behind.

31

THE NEW CHESTNUT TREE

Time 4/4. Tempo 30/32.
Music: 'Underneath the Spreading Chestnut Tree'.
Man's steps. Lady normal opposite.
Commence in Double Hold with man facing wall.

Bar	Count	L AND R SWAYS - CHEST*NUT*TREE ACTION - L & R SWAYS - CLAP OWN HANDS 3 TIMES
1	SS	LF to side and sway L, RF in place; sway to R, LF in place then release hands.
2	QQS	Place hands on own chest; place hands on head (or forehead); raise arms, outspread above head, lower hands then rejoin in Double Hold.
3	SS	Repeat L and R sways as bar 1 releasing hands.
4	QQS	Clap own hands 3 times in time to QQS almost at shoulder height. Rejoin hands in Double Hold, still face wall and partner.

OPEN RUN TO L AND R - L AND R SWAYS - CHEST*NUT*TREE ACTION

Bar	Count	
5	QQS	Turning slightly outward to PP, hands still joined - LF to side along LOD; RF fwd and across in PP along LOD; LF to side along LOD and swivel inward to R (lady to L) to face against LOD in counter PP still Double Hold.
6	QQS	RF to side against LOD in counter PP; LF fwd and across against LOD; RF to side against LOD and swivel inward to L (lady to R), end facing wall and partner.
7	SS	Repeat L and R sways as bar 1 releasing hands.
8	QQS	Repeat Chest*Nut*Tree action as bar 2.

L & R SWAYS - CLAP OWN HANDS 3 TIMES - L & R SWAYS - CLAP LADY'S HANDS 3 TIMES

Bar	Count	
9	SS	Repeat bar 1, L and R sways.
10	QQS	Clap own hands 3 times as bar 4.
11	SS	Repeat bar 1, L and R sways.
12	QQS	Clap partner's hands 3 times using palms of hands held vertical almost shoulder height, rejoin hands in Double Hold, man facing wall.
13-16	---	Repeat bars 5-8, runs, sways, Chest*Nut*Tree action.

JIVE CHASSÉS ALONG LOD - OPEN RUN - JIVE CHASSÉS AGAINST LOD - OPEN RUN

17	Q&Q	LF to side along LOD; half close RF to LF; LF
	Q&Q	to side along LOD and repeat on RLR.
18	QQS	Repeat Open Run to L to end fcg against LOD. LRL.
19	Q&Q	Repeat Jive Chassé against LOD commencing RF.
	Q&Q	RLR, LRL.
20	QQS	Repeat Open Run to R to end facing wall and partner in Double Hold. Release hold.

SOLO WALKS TO CENTRE AND TO PARTNER - L AND R SWAYS - CHEST*NUTS ACTION

21	QQS	LF back to centre (lady RF back to wall); RF back to centre; LF back to centre (check).
22	QSS	RF fwd to wall and partner (lady fwd RF to centre); LF fwd to wall; RF fwd to wall and partner taking Double Hold, LF closing without weight.
23	SS	Repeat bar 1, L and R sways and release hold.
24	SS	Place hands on own chest; place hands on head (or forehead). (Only 2 actions.) Partners shout "**Chest-Nuts**" in time to Slow, Slow.
25-32	---	Repeat bars 1-8. Rejoin hands in Double Hold, face wall and partner.

To make progressive: In bar 22 man moves L to next partner in front.

This dance is based on the original 'Chestnut Tree' arranged by Adèle England and C. L. Heiman in 1938.

A dashing young man from Granada
Was eager to learn the Lambada
Though he bent and he swayed
Little progress was mayed
He needs to try harder and hada.

CELEBRATION JIVE

Time 4/4. Tempo 36.
Man's steps. Lady counterpart unless otherwise stated.
Commence in Double Hold, man facing wall and partner.

Bar	Count	**JIVE CHASSÉS - STEP AND DOUBLE TAP ALONG LOD - PROM ZIG-ZAG - STEP AND DOUBLE TAP**
1	Q&Q	Jive chassé to L along LOD; jive chassé to R
	Q&Q	against LOD, RLR, turning slightly outward, face DW (lady face DC).
2	SQQ	LF to side along LOD, Double Hold in PP; tap RF twice at side of LF.
3	QQQQ	RF fwd and across along LOD turning R (lady to L); LF to side along LOD, partners almost square; RF back under body DC turning L (lady LF back under body DW turning R); LF to side along LOD still Double Hold in PP.
4	SQQ	RF fwd and across along LOD; tap LF twice at side of RF.

STEP, POINTS - SWIVEL, POINT, SWIVEL, POINT - REARWARD WALKS/KICKS - FALLAWAY 4 STEP

5	QQQQ	LF to side along LOD, Double Hold in PP; point RF fwd and across along LOD; RF fwd and across along LOD; point LF to side along LOD, all short steps.
6	QQQQ	LF to side along LOD and swivel R (lady swivel L); point RF to side against LOD in counter PP; extend RF slightly against LOD and swivel L (lady to R) to face along LOD; point LF to side along LOD, wt held back.
7	QQQQ	LF back against LOD in CBMP and fallaway; kick RF fwd along LOD, knee bent; close RF back to LF; kick LF fwd, knee bent.
8	QQQQ	LF back against LOD in CBMP and fallaway turning R (lady to L); RF to side against LOD, face wall and partner, still turning slightly; LF fwd and across against LOD in Counter Double Hold turning to L (lady to R); close RF to LF facing slightly DC along LOD (lady face slightly DW) preparing for solo outward turns.

34

SOLO OUTWARD TURN - FWD LOCK AND TAP
- SOLO INWARD TURN - FWD LOCK AND TAP

9   QQQQ LF fwd towards DC releasing hold commencing to turn L (lady to R); RF to side still turning: LF back along LOD joining inside hands, lady's R hand in man's L hand; cross RF loosely in front of LF (lady LF in front of RF) without weight.

10 Q&QS RF fwd against LOD; lock LF behind RF; extend RF fwd against LOD, short steps; tap LF at side of RF.

11 QQQQ LF fwd against LOD commencing to turn L (lady to R); RF to side across LOD still turning and release hold; LF back against LOD joining inside hands, lady's L hand in man's R hand; cross RF loosely in front of LF (lady RF in front of LF) without weight.

12 Q&QS RF fwd along LOD; lock LF behind RF; extend RF fwd along LOD, short steps; tap LF at side of RF taking Double Hold in PP.

SWIVEL, POINT, SWIVEL, POINT - STEP, DRAG
- DIAG WALKS - FWD WALKS TO PARTNER

13 QQQQ Repeat swivel, points as bar 6.

14 SS   LF to side along LOD, wide step, relaxing knee; drag RF to LF straightening legs tng sltly outwards to face LOD (dancers may go "OOO-OOH" during this bar).

15 QQQQ LF diag fwd towards DC releasing hold (lady RF diag fwd towards DW); RF fwd and across; LF diag fwd DC and swivel R to face wall and partner (lady swivel L on RF); close RF to LF and clap own hands.

16 QQQQ LF fwd towards wall and partner (lady RF fwd); RF fwd to partner; LF fwd; RF to LF taking Double Hold in commencing position.

To make progressive: In bar 16 man veers to L to next partner on L; lady will also veer to L to next partner on L.

Remember not to drink and jive.

ISLAND CALYPSO

Time 4/4. Tempo 36. Music: 'Island of Dreams'.
Man's steps. Lady counterpart unless otherwise stated.
Commences in ballroom hold, man facing LOD.

Bar	Count	HALF SQUARE - SIDE POINT AND CLOSE - REARWARD HALF SQUARE - SIDE POINT AND CLOSE
1	SQQ	LF fwd dn LOD; RF to side to wall; LF closes to RF.
2	SS	Point RF to side to wall; close RF to LF without weight.
3	SQQ	RF back against LOD; LF to side to centre; close RF to LF, still face LOD.
4	SS	Point LF to side to centre; close LF to RF without weight.

TURNING CHASSÉS TO L AND R - STEP, POINT - STEP, POINT TO PP

5	SQQ	LF fwd down LOD, slight turn to L; RF diag fwd down LOD; close LF to RF, face towards DC.
6	SQQ	RF diag fwd down LOD, slight turn to R; LF fwd down LOD; close RF to LF face LOD still in ballroom hold.
7	SS	LF fwd down LOD, slight turn L; point RF fwd down LOD, only short steps.
8	SS	RF fwd down LOD, slight turn to R and turning lady to PP; point LF to side along LOD in PP, only short steps.

PROMENADE WALKS AND CHECK - FALLAWAY WALKS AND AERIALS - FALLAWAY TWINKLE - PROMENADE ROCK

9	SS	LF to side along LOD in PP; RF fwd along LOD relaxing knee, check (chair).
10	SS	LF back against LOD in fallaway and raising RF to low fwd aerial (S); RF back against LOD in fallaway and raising LF to low fwd aerial (S).
11	QQS	LF back in fallaway; close RF to LF; LF to side along LOD in PP.
12	QQS	Rock fwd on RF, small step; rock rearward on LF; extend RF fwd along LOD.

36

CALYPSO RUN IN PP - CALYPSO RUN IN CPP - PROM SWAYS - FALLAWAY AND SLIP PIVOT

13   QQQQ   LF to side along LOD in PP; RF fwd and across along LOD in PP; LF to side along LOD in PP and swivel inward to R (lady to L) to counter PP facing against LOD; flick (or kick) RF against LOD, do not kick high (Calypso Run).

14   QQQQ   RF to side against LOD in counter PP; LF fwd and across against LOD; RF to side against LOD and swivel inward to L (lady to R) to face LOD in PP; flick LF to side along LOD, keep foot fairly low (Calypso Run).

15   SS   LF to side and fwd along LOD, sway fwd, RF in place; transfer weight to RF and sway to R and rearward preparing to step back on LF in fallaway.

16   QQQQ   LF back against LOD in CBMP and fallaway; RF back against LOD (lady pivot on RF then LF fwd square to man) bringing lady in line; side LF to centre; close RF to LF facing LOD in commencing hold and position.

DOUGLAS DI LEMMA (Galop Grotesque)

Arranged by Isa Bogus.
Winner DAFT Competition - Oldham 1931.
Time: Midnight. Tempo: One degree under.
Normal hold gent facing down LOD, L hand holding lady's L waist. Both partners right arms crooked at 45°.

1.	*Commence with whisk.*	*QQQQ*
2.	*Basic step fwd diag wall, gents LF and RF in unison. Lady reverse.*	*QQQ*
3.	*Half natural turn leading L.S, R leg with thigh and calf at 45°.*	*SSQQ*
4.	*Draw LF behind RF, arms outstretched parallel to floor and spin 22 times. Lady grasps man's waist firmly until descent. Rise and fall on 13th spin.*	*QQSS*

(Remaining 28 bars lost)

37

RAINBOW RAG

Time 4/4. Tempo 46/48.
Man's steps. Lady counterpart unless otherwise stated.
Commence inside hands joined in Open Hold, partners facing along LOD.

Bar	Count	WALKS - LOCK STEP - STEP, POINT - LOCK STEP
1	SS	LF fwd along LOD; RF fwd along LOD.
2	QQS	LF diag fwd; RF crosses behind LF; LF diag fwd along LOD.
3	SS	RF fwd along LOD; point LF fwd along LOD.
4	QQS	LF diag fwd along LOD; RF crosses behind LF; LF diag fwd along LOD.

		PROMENADE ZIG-ZAG - INWARD TURN - DOUBLE CHASSÉ AGAINST LOD
5	SS	Taking Double Hold in PP, RF fwd and across in PP and CBMP turning inward to R (lady turns R); LF to side along LOD facing wall and partner still turning slightly R (lady to L).
6	SS	RF back in CBMP DC turning to L (lady LF back DW tng R) - LF to side along LOD still PP Double Hold.
7	SS	RF fwd and across along LOD turning inward to R (lady turns L); LF closes to RF facing wall and partner.
8	QQQQ	RF to side against LOD; LF closes to RF; RF to side against LOD; LF closes to RF facing wall and partner.

		STEP, SWING - INWARD TURN TO PP - PROM SCOOP - TWINKLE AND LOCK STEP
9	SS	RF to side against LOD, slight turn outward; swing LF fwd and across against LOD to low aerial.
10	SS	LF fwd and across against LOD turning to L (lady to R); RF closes to LF in PP, partners facing along LOD, releasing lady's R hand.
11	SS	Side and fwd along LOD in PP, wide step; drag RF to LF with a drag action, slight outward body turn.
12	QQQQ	LF back in fallaway against LOD; RF closes to LF; LF diag fwd along LOD; RF closes to LF in PP, partners facing along LOD in PP.

NAT PROM TURN TO BACK LOD - FALLAWAY AND SLIP PIVOT - FOUR STEP

13	SS	LF to side along LOD in PP; RF fwd in PP and CBMP DW turning to (lady no turn).
14	SS	LF to side and slightly back, backing LOD turning slightly L (lady RF fwd down LOD between partner's feet turning R); RF diag down LOD with LF brushing to RF in PP (lady on last step LF diag back along LOD with RF brushing back to LF in PP).
15	SS	LF back in CBMP and fallaway along LOD; RF back along LOD with lady square (lady pivoting to L on RF, slips LF fwd in line with man).
16	QQQQ	LF fwd in CBMP DW against LOD in line turning to L; RF to side and slightly back, backing DC against LOD; LF back in CBMP DC against LOD (lady RF fwd OP turning to R); RF closes to LF, partners in PP facing along LOD releasing hold and joining inside hands as at commencement.

More Hints from Professor Dan Shoo

7.   An open telemark can be made more enjoyable by making a strong sway towards the bar on the third step (position held until it's your turn to pay).

8.   Avoid 'bounce' rhythm with the contra cheque.

9.   Tighten up your brush tap or you will be considered a 'drip'.

10.   Do not attempt a feather finish if your feet are ticklish.

11.   In the zig-zag make sure that you don't dance the 'zag' before the 'zig'. Otherwise you will find yourself moving rapidly backward with the lady hanging on to you.

12.   When performing a lock step make sure that the music is in the right 'key'.

THE JINGLE JIVE

Time 4/4. Tempo 34/36.
Music: 'Jingle Bell Rock', sequence jives.
Man's steps given. Lady's steps contra.
Commence partners facing LOD, inside hands joined, the free hand held at shoulder level.

Bar Count

1   1234   LF fwd and slightly side along LOD; swing RF diag fwd across with a kicking action.
RF fwd and slightly side along LOD; swing LF diag fwd across RF with a kicking action.

2   1234   LF fwd along LOD, short step turning to face DC (lady turns to face DW); tap RF at side of LF turning to face LOD; RF fwd along LOD turning to face DW (lady face DC); tap LF at side of RF, short step.

3   1234   Turning to face LOD, LF to side and fwd moving DC (lady DW) releasing hold; RF fwd across LF; side and fwd LF moving DC body facing LOD; tap RF behind LF swaying L from the waist and tapping RF behind LF, toe pointing downward, headline to L. As R toe is tapped, relax L knee and clap.

4   1234   Correcting sway, body turn to R, RF fwd towards wall and partner (lady moving towards centre and partner); LF fwd; RF fwd towards wall and partner; close LF to RF taking Double Hold.

5   1234   The feet remain in place during this bar.
Sway to L (bending at waist), headline to L (lady to R) lowering L hand (clasped with lady's R hand) about 4" with a jerking movement (count 1); quickly raise hands to original position and repeat the jerking movement, body still bent at waist (2); straightening body repeat jerking movement of counts 1 and 2 swaying to R, headline to R, using R hand clasped in lady's L hand. End weight on RF preparing to move to L.

6	1234	Correcting sway and headline, side LF along LOD facing wall and partner still in Double Hold; close RF to LF; LF to side along LOD turning slightly to R (lady to L); close RF to LF without weight now facing DW against LOD (lady DC against LOD).
7	1234	RF to side against LOD in Double Hold, small step; kick LF fwd across RF; place LF at side of RF slightly apart; kick RF fwd DW against LOD.
8	1234	RF back DC down LOD turning to L (lady LF back DW turning to R); side and fwd LF along LOD releasing lady's R hand; RF fwd along LOD in Open Hold; close LF to RF without weight in commencing hold and position.

To make progressive: Man veers to L in bar 4 towards next partner in front; lady veers to L towards next partner behind.

LET'S STROLL

Time 4/4. Tempo 28/30.
Music: 'Underneath the Arches', 'Meet Me at the Corner', songs that dancers can sing to.
*Man and lady dance the **same steps** throughout.*
Commence facing LOD, in Shadow Hold, or link arms.

Bar	Count	WALKS - CHECKS DW AND DC - STEP AND POINT
1	SS	Both partners LF fwd along LOD; RF fwd along LOD.
2	SQQ	LF fwd across RF towards DW (check); transfer weight back to RF, face LOD; LF to side, very short step, almost closed to RF with weight.
3	SQQ	RF fwd across LF towards DC (check); transfer weight back to LF, face LOD; RF to side, very short step almost closed to LF with weight.
4	SS	LF fwd along LOD; point RF fwd along LOD, short step.

LET'S STROLL (continued)

WALKS - CHECKS DC AND DW - STEP AND POINT

5   SS   RF fwd along LOD; LF fwd along LOD.

6   SQQ   RF fwd across LF towards DC (check); transfer weight back to LF, face LOD; RF to side, very short step almost closed to LF with weight.

7   SQQ   LF fwd across RF towards DW (check); transfer weight back to RF, face LOD; LF to side, very short step almost closed to RF with weight.

8   SS   RF fwd along LOD; point LF fwd along LOD, short step.

FWD WALKS - REARWARD WALKS AND AERIALS - SLIGHTLY DIAG CHASSÉS

9   SS   LF fwd along LOD; RF fwd along LOD, relax knee (check).

10   SS   LF back against LOD raising RF to low fwd aerial (S); RF back against LOD raising LF to low aerial (S) (check).

11   QQS   LF fwd slightly DC; RF almost closes to LF; LF fwd slightly DC.

12   QQS   RF fwd slightly DW, LF almost closes to RF; RF fwd slightly DW.

Face LOD during bars 11 and 12.

SWAY L AND CLOSE - SWAY R AND CLOSE - L AND R SWAYS

13   SQQ   LF to side to centre and sway L, RF in place; transfer weight to RF; LF closes to RF.

14   SQQ   RF to side to wall and sway R, LF in place; transfer weight to LF; RF closes to LF.

15   SS   LF to side to centre and sway L, RF in place; sway to R towards wall, LF in place.

16   SS   Sway to L towards centre, RF in place; slight sway to R on RF closing LF to RF without weight. Face LOD.

Note: May also be danced as a Trio with a lady on either side of man, arms linked, or in 2's, 4's, 6's or more depending on the size of the dance hall.

GOOD WISHES WALTZ (Modern)

Time 3/4. Tempo 30.
Man's steps. Lady counterpart unless otherwise stated.
Commence in Ballroom Hold, man facing DC.

Bar	Count	REVERSE TURN TO PP - STEP, POINTS IN PP (Double Hold)

REVERSE TURN TO PP - STEP, POINTS IN PP (Double Hold)

1   LF fwd DC commence to turn to L; RF to side backing DW still turning; close LF to RF backing LOD.

2   RF back down LOD turning to L (no turn for lady); LF to side along LOD in PP; close RF to LF still in PP but change to Double Hold.

3   LF to side along LOD (1); swing RF fwd along LOD to low aerial (2); point RF to floor (3).

4   RF fwd and across along LOD (1); swing LF to side along LOD (2); point LF to floor (3).

TURNING CLOSED CHANGES - STEP, POINTS IN PP (Double Hold)

5   LF to side, releasing front hands and turning outward to L (lady turn to R); RF diag fwd along LOD; close LF to RF facing towards DC (lady face DW), partners in Open Hold.

6   RF diag fwd along LOD turning inward to R (lady turn to L); LF to side along LOD; close RF to LF and adopt Double Hold in PP.

7   Repeat bar 3 (step, point).

8   Repeat bar 4 (step, point).

CHECKED FALLAWAY WALKS - TURNING HOVERS TO R AND L - DOUBLE RONDÉ IN PP

9   Still in Double Hold, LF back in CBMP and fallaway against LOD; RF diag back against LOD; LF back in CBMP and fallaway against LOD (check).

10   RF fwd and across along LOD turning inward to R (lady to L) rising and commencing turning hover; LF to side along LOD still rising and turning slightly; transfer weight fwd and slightly side now facing against LOD in Contra PP, Double Hold.

11	LF fwd and across against LOD turning inward to L (lady to R) commencing turning hover and rising; RF to side against LOD still rising and turning slightly; transfer weight fwd and slightly side to LF now facing along LOD.
12	RF fwd and across along LOD; rondé LF fwd and outward crossing loosely in front of RF **without weight**; rondé LF back in fallaway and CBMP, loosely cross LF behind RF **with weight**. Adopt PP hold, partners facing along LOD.

CHASSÉ FROM PP - NATURAL SPIN TURN - 456 REVERSE TURN

13	RF fwd and across along LOD in PP turning lady square; LF to side and slightly fwd; RF closes to LF facing DW; LF to side and slightly fwd (1.2&3).
14	RF fwd in CBMP OP DW commence to turn to R; LF to side backing DC still turning; RF closes to LF backing LOD.
15	LF back, backing LOD and pivot to R; RF fwd in CBMP facing LOD continue to turn R. LF to side and slightly back, backing DC **against** LOD (underturned).
16	RF back DC against LOD turning to L; LF to side and slightly fwd pointing DC; close RF to LF facing DC.

To make progressive: Bars 3/4 or bars 7/8 may be used. Man releases hold and step, points fwd to next partner, lady remaining in place awaiting next partner from behind. Alternatively lady could make progression, man remaining in place. All progressions may be used during the sequence.

This lady the wrong side of forty,
Was trying to dance the back corté,
But she wasn't so neat,
And she flattened his feet,
And her partner yelled, "Stop that, it's naughty."

(At least that's what he said when the swear words were deleted.)

DARKTOWN RAG

Time 4/4. Tempo 46/48.
Man's steps. Lady counterpart unless otherwise stated.
Commence in Ballroom Hold, man facing LOD.

Bar	Count	**WALKS - 123 REVERSE TURN - STEP, POINTS**
1	SS	LF fwd down LOD; RF fwd down LOD.
2	SQQ	LF fwd sltly DC commencing to turn to L; RF to side backing DW still tng; LF closes to RF backing LOD.
3	SS	RF back down LOD; point LF back.
4	SS	LF fwd closing to RF with weight; point RF to side, short step, face against LOD.

WALKS AGAINST LOD - 123 NATURAL TURN - STEP, POINTS

5	SS	RF fwd against LOD; LF fwd against LOD.
6	SQQ	RF fwd slightly DC against LOD commencing to turn to R; LF to side backing DW against LOD still turning; RF closes to LF backing against LOD.
7	SS	LF back against LOD; point RF back.
8	SS	RF fwd closing to LF with weight; point LF to side, short step, face down LOD.

DIAGONAL CHASSÉS DC AND DW - STEP, POINT FORWARD AND REARWARD

9	QQS	LF diag fwd down LOD; RF closes to LF; LF diag fwd down LOD. Face LOD during chassé.
10	QQS	RF diag fwd down LOD; LF closes to RF; RF diag fwd down LOD. Face LOD during chassé.
11	SS	LF fwd down LOD; point RF fwd down LOD, check. May be danced with a Charleston action.
12	SQQ	RF back against LOD; point LF back against LOD. May be danced with a Charleston action.

CROSS SWIVEL - FISHTAIL WITH EXTRA LOCK STEP

13	SS	LF fwd in CBMP OP DW and swivel to L; RF closes to LF without weight facing DC, partner slightly on man's R side.

DARKTOWN RAG (continued)

14   SS   RF fwd in CBMP OP DC, checking step; replace weight back to LF swaying slightly rearward.

15   SQQ   Extend RF fwd slightly in CBMP OP commencing to turn R; LF crosses behind RF, sway R, face LOD; RF fwd and slightly to side face LOD.

16   QQQQ   LF diag fwd down LOD; RF crosses behind LF; LF diag fwd down LOD; RF crosses behind LF, face LOD.

THE JIVE-A-LONG

Time 4/4. Tempo 36/38. Music: Sequence jives.
Man's steps. Lady counterpart unless otherwise stated.
Commence in Double Hold, man facing wall and partner.

Bar	Count	JIVE CHASSÉS TO L AND R - CURVING WALKS TO CHANGE OF PLACES
1	1&2	LF to side along LOD; RF part closes towards
	3&4	LF; LF to side along LOD, short steps; RF to side against LOD; LF part closes towards RF; RF to side against LOD, short steps, turn slightly to L on second chassé to end facing DW, lady backing but slightly on man's R.
2	1234	Keeping hold, LF fwd DW commencing to curve to R PO (lady RF fwd OP DC against LOD commencing to curve R); RF fwd towards wall still curving; LF to side facing DC against LOD, slight swivel R; RF closes to LF facing centre and partner, now in opposite places, (lady RF fwd OP DC against LOD commencing to curve to R; LF fwd towards centre still curving; RF fwd DC turning to R; LF closes to RF facing wall and partner). Partners still in Double Hold.

JIVE CHASSÉS TO L AND R - CURVING WALKS TO CHANGE OF PLACES

3	1&2	Repeat Jive chassé as Bar 1 commencing man
	3&4	facing centre, lady backing still in Double Hold, end facing DC against LOD.

46

| 4 | 1234 | Repeat bar 2, curving walks, back to own places end man fcg DW, lady fcg DC, release lady's R hand. Join inside hands in Open Hold, ready to move along LOD. |

FWD JIVE LOCKS AND RELEASE HOLD - DIAG SOLO WALKS AND CLAP HANDS

5	1&2	LF diag fwd along LOD; RF crosses loosely
	3&4	behind LF; LF diag fwd; RF diag fwd along LOD; LF crosses loosely behind RF; RF diag fwd along LOD, all small steps.
6	1234	LF diag fwd towards DC (lady towards DW) releasing hold; RF fwd across LF moving DC; LF diag fwd towards DC, slight swivel to R; clap hands on 4th count facing wall and partner, feet slightly apart.

FWD WALKS TO PARTNER - BOOGIE POINTS IN DOUBLE HOLD

| 7 | 1234 | RF fwd towards wall and partner (lady LF fwd towards centre and partner); LF fwd towards partner; RF fwd to partner; LF closes to RF without weight (or slight tap) taking Double Hold facing wall and partner. |
| 8 | 1234 | Point LF towards DW (lady points RF towards DC), slight body turn outwards, headlines towards pointing foot; LF closes back to RF with weight, face wall and partner; point RF towards DW against LOD (lady points LF DC against LOD); slight body turn outwards, headlines towards pointing foot; RF closes back to LF with weight facing wall and partner in commencing hold and position. |

To make progressive: In bar 7 man moves leftwards to next partner in front, lady moves leftwards to partner behind.

It's good to dance - don't waste music - dance to it!
It's a long lane that has no sequence dances at the end of it.

GOOD-WILL SAUNTER

Time 4/4. Tempo 28.
Man's steps. Lady counterpart unless otherwise stated.
Commence in ballroom hold, man facing LOD.

Bar	Count	WALKS AND SWIVELS TO R SIDE, CHECK - REARWARD TWINKLE AND FWD LOCK - PP ENDING
1	SS	LF fwd down LOD; RF fwd down LOD, slight swivel to R, brushing LF to RF, end facing DW.
2	SS	LF fwd in CBMP OP DW and swivel to L to face DC brushing RF to LF; RF fwd in CBMP OP DC, R hip to R hip (check).
3	QQQQ	Transfer weight back to LF, slight turn R; RF closes to LF, face LOD, lady in line; LF diag fwd down LOD; RF crosses behind LF.
4	SS	LF fwd down LOD, slight turn L; RF diag fwd down LOD and swivel L to face against LOD (lady no turn), partners in PP facing against LOD.

		ZIG-ZAG TO R SIDE, CHECK - REARWARD TWINKLE AND FWD LOCK - PP ENDING
5	SQQ	LF to side against LOD in PP; RF fwd and across in PP and CBMP facing DC against LOD turning R (lady no turn); LF to side and slightly back against LOD almost facing partner still turning slightly R.
6	QQS	RF back in CBMP DW against LOD, PO on L side, turning to L; LF diag fwd against LOD, face partner; RF fwd in CBMP OP DW against LOD (check).
7	QQQQ	Transfer weight back to LF, slight turn R; RF closes to LF, lady in line, face against LOD; LF diag fwd against LOD; RF crosses behind LF.
8	SS	LF fwd against LOD, lady in line, slight turn L; RF diag fwd against LOD and swivel L to face LOD, partners now in PP facing towards LOD.

		FWD AND REARWARD SWAYS IN OPEN HOLD - SIDE SOLO CHASSÉS - FWD WALKS TO PP
9	SS	Taking Double Hold, LF to side along LOD in PP; releasing front hands, RF fwd and across along LOD, sway fwd, swing clasped hands fwd in Open Hold, man facing DC, lady facing DW.

10	SS	Sway rearward on LF; transfer weight fwd to RF closing LF to RF without weight.
11	QQS	Releasing hold, LF to side towards centre (lady RF to side towards wall); RF closes to LF; LF to side towards centre turning inwards to R (lady to L). End partners facing each other and clap own hands.
12	QQS	RF fwd towards wall and partner; LF fwd; RF fwd with slight outward turn closing LF without weight. Retake Double Hold in PP.

STEP, POINTS IN DOUBLE HOLD - FWD AND REARWARD BALANCÉ - NATURAL ROTARY CHASSÉ

13	QQQQ	LF to side along LOD, Double Hold in PP; point RF fwd and across along LOD; RF fwd and across along LOD; point LF to side along LOD.
14	SS	LF to side along LOD, Balancé movement with RF closing behind LF without weight; RF back against LOD, Balancé movement, turn slightly R (lady no turn); LF closes to RF without weight facing lady, back DC.
15	QQS	LF to side towards DW commencing to turn R, Ballroom Hold; RF closes to LF, backing LOD; LF back commencing to turn R.
16	QQS	RF to side along LOD still turning R; LF closes to RF still turning; RF fwd down LOD with LF closing without weight.

To make progressive: Man veers to L in bar 12 to next partner in front, lady veering L to next partner behind.

> *She wasn't much good in a saunter,*
> *And her friends would ridicule and taunt her.*
> *But try as she might*
> *No thing would go right*
> *And her efforts would come back to haunt her.*
>
> *Don't dance a whisk with an egg in your pocket*
> *otherwise the yolk may be on you.*

THE PARTY-MIX

Time 4/4. Tempo 30-34. Jives or Barn Dance medleys.
Commence in Double Hold, man facing wall and lady.
Man's steps. Lady normal opposite.

Bar	Count	JIVE CHASSÉS TO L AND R - 3 WALKS - JIVE CHASSÉS TO R AND L - 3 WALKS
1	Q&Q Q&Q	LF to side along LOD; almost close RF to LF; LF to side along LOD; RF to side against LOD; almost close LF to RF; RF to side against LOD, all short steps.
2	QQS	Turning slightly outwards, LF to side along LOD; RF fwd and across along LOD; LF to side along LOD turning inwards to face wall and partner.
3-4	---	Repeat the pattern of bars 1 and 2 commencing RF and moving against LOD. End facing wall and partner.

		SIDE CHASSÉ TO L AND SWING - SIDE CHASSÉ TO R AND SWING - STEP, POINTS
5	QQQQ	Still in Double Hold, LF to side along LOD, face wall; close RF to LF; LF to side along LOD; swing RF fwd and across along LOD to low aerial.
6	QQQQ	RF to side against LOD; close LF to RF; RF to side against LOD, swing LF fwd and across against LOD to low aerial.
7	QQQQ	LF to side along LOD; swing RF fwd and across LF to low aerial; RF to side against LOD; swing LF fwd and across against LOD to low aerial turning to PP in Double Hold.
8	QQQQ	LF to side along LOD; point RF fwd and across along LOD; RF fwd and across along LOD; point LF to side along LOD, body sways on the point.

		JIVE CHASSÉS ALONG LOD - STEP AND DOUBLE TAP - REPEAT ON OPPOSITE FOOT
9	Q&Q	In loose Double Hold, jive chassé fwd along LOD, LRL; repeat on opposite foot, RLR.
10	SQQ	LF to side and fwd along LOD, checking step, weight held fwd, leaving RF in place; tap RF twice at side of LF.

11	Q&Q	Repeat the jive chassés along LOD on opposite foot;
	Q&Q	RLR, LRL.
12	SQQ	RF fwd and across along LOD, checking step, weight held fwd, weight on RF; tap LF twice at side of RF.

SIDE SOLO WALKS - FWD SOLO WALKS - PAS DE BASQUE TO L AND R - POINT, CLOSES

13	QQS	LF to side towards centre releasing Double Hold (lady side RF towards wall); RF fwd and across LF moving sideways; LF to side and slightly fwd towards centre turning R to face wall and partner then clap own hands.
14	QQS	RF fwd towards wall and partner (lady LF fwd); LF fwd; RF fwd, again taking Double Hold with LF brushing to RF.
15	Q&Q	Pas de Basque to L along LOD, LRL, small steps.
	Q&Q	Pas de Basque to R against LOD, RLR, small steps.
16	QQQQ	Point LF diag fwd towards DW (lady point DC); close LF back to RF; point RF diag fwd towards DW against LOD; close RF back to LF.

To make progressive: In bar 14 man moves leftwards to partner in front, lady moves leftwards to partner behind.

SWINGTIME BLUES

Time 4/4. Tempo 44/46.
Man's steps. Lady counterpart unless otherwise stated.
Man and lady facing LOD, inside hands joined in Open Hold.

Bar	Count	WALKS - FORWARD LOCKSTEP - FORWARD AND REARWARD POINTS - STEP, CLOSE
1	SS	LF fwd along LOD; RF fwd along LOD.
2	QQS	LF diag fwd along LOD; RF crosses behind LF; LF diag fwd.
3	SS	RF fwd along LOD; point LF fwd along LOD, body leans backwards.
4	SQQ	Point LF back against LOD, body leans fwd; LF diag fwd along LOD; RF closes to LF taking promenade hold and position.

51

NATURAL PROMENADE TURN - STEP, SWING ALONG LOD - STEP, SWING AGAINST LOD

5	SS	LF to side along LOD in PP; RF fwd and across towards DW commencing to turn R (lady no turn).
6	SS	LF to side and slightly back, backing LOD (lady RF fwd between man's feet) and pivot to R; RF fwd down LOD turning lady to PP.
7	SS	Taking Double Hold in PP, LF to side along LOD;
8	SS	swing RF fwd to low aerial along LOD; turning inwards to R (lady to L); RF to side against LOD still Double Hold; swing RF fwd against LOD.

INWARDS TURN AND SCOOP - SOLO CHASSÉS TO CENTRE AND TO WALL AND PARTNER

9	SS	LF fwd against LOD turning L (lady turns R); RF closes to LF facing towards LOD.
10	SS	LF to side along LOD, wide step, knee relaxed; RF closes to LF with a dragging action, making a slight outward turn to face LOD.
11	QQS	Releasing hold, LF to side to centre (lady RF to side to wall); RF closes to LF; LF to side towards centre, relaxing knee (check).
12	QQS	RF to side towards wall and partner; LF closes to RF; RF to side joining inside hands in Open Hold, partners facing LOD.

OUTWARD TURN - BACK TO BACK SWAYS - INWARD TURN TO FACE LOD

13	SQQ	LF fwd along LOD turning L (lady to R); RF to side along LOD; LF closes to RF, partners almost back to back, front hands still joined.
14	SS	RF to side along LOD swaying to R; sway to L on LF.
15	SS	Repeat bar 14, R and L sways. All sways may be danced 'jauntily'.
16	SQQ	Extend RF to side turning slightly R; LF diag fwd along LOD; RF closes to LF facing towards LOD in commencing position and hold.

To make progressive: In bar 12 man moves diag to wall to next partner in front. Lady may move slightly back to next partner.

JINGLE JINKS

Time 4/4. Tempo 46/48.
Man's steps. Lady counterpart unless otherwise stated.
Commence in Open Hold (as Mayfair Quickstep).

Bar	Count	WALKS - OPEN CHASSÉS (SKIPPING ACTION) - STEP, POINT
1	SS	LF fwd along LOD, inside hands joined (lady RF fwd); RF fwd along LOD.
2	QQS	LF fwd along LOD; RF part closes to LF; extend LF fwd along LOD.
3	QQS	RF fwd along LOD; LF part closes to RF; extend RF fwd along LOD.
4	SS	LF fwd along LOD; point RF along LOD.

PROMENADE TWIST - STEP, POINT - STEP, SWING ALONG LOD - STEP, SWING AGAINST LOD

5	SS	RF fwd along LOD turning inwards to R (lady to L); LF closes to RF with weight, partners almost square. Take Double Hold.
6	SS	Tng outwards to PP, Double Hold, RF fwd and across along LOD; point LF to side, almost closed to RF.
7	SS	LF to side along LOD, relax knee slightly; swing RF fwd and across along LOD to low aerial, very little body turn.
8	SS	Turning to face partner and wall, RF to side agst LOD, short step, relaxing knee slightly; swing LF fwd and across against LOD to low aerial, very little body turn.

SIDE, CLOSES - ARM JERKS WITH SWAYS

9	SS	Still Double Hold, man facing wall and partner, LF to side along LOD, wide step, arms swinging to L; RF closes to LF, arms back to normal position.
10	SS	Repeat last bar (bar 9).
11	QQS	With partners still facing each other in Double Hold, sway to L from waist jerking the clasped hands down and up 3 times to the timing (only man's L and lady's R arms used). Headlines along LOD.

| 12 | QQS | Repeat last bar but sway to R from waist jerking arms down and up 3 times to the timing (man's R and lady's L arms used). Heads turning to face against LOD, feet in place for bars 11 and 12. |

WALKS IN PP AND CHECK - INWARDS TURN - HAND CLAPS - OWN HAND CLAPS

13	SS	LF to side along LOD in Double Hold; releasing front hands; RF fwd and across along LOD, inside hands joined, relaxing knee (check).
14	SS	Transfer weight back to LF turning inwards to R (lady to L); slide RF to side against LOD, short step, facing wall and partner and releasing hold.
15	QQQQ	Slap palm of L hand against lady's L palm and repeat (QQ); slap palm of R hand against palm of lady's R hand and repeat (QQ).
16	QQS	Clap own hands 3 times (lady will clap her hands) (QQS).

First step of each following sequence will be diagonally fwd as partners turn outwards to face LOD joining inside hands.

To make progressive: Lady will remain in place for bars 9 and 10, man making his normal movement to lady in front. Rejoin hands for the arm jerks and sways.

There was a young man came from 'Frisco
Who tried various steps at the disco.
He was going real strong
When the cramp came along
And for weeks had his legs locked, that is so.

Although the sprain scarce stands the strain
And dancing feet makes blunders
Do not despair re wear and tear,
A transplant will work wonders.

NINETIES SWING

Time 4/4. Tempo 46/48.
Man's steps. Lady counterpart unless otherwise state
Commence in Ballroom Hold, man facing LOD.

Bar	Count	STEP, POINTS TO PP - PROMENADE CHASSÉ - INWARDS SWIVEL AND TAP
1	SS	LF fwd down LOD, very slight turn to L; point RF diag fwd down LOD.
2	SS	RF diag fwd down LOD, slight turn to R and turning lady to PP; point LF to side along LOD in PP.
3	QQS	LF to side along LOD in PP; RF closes to LF; LF to side along LOD in PP.
4	SS	RF fwd and across in PP and CBMP along LOD and swivel to R (lady to L); tap LF at side of RF, short step, face wall and partner.

		FOUR STEP TO PP - SIDE AND SWING ALONG LOD - SIDE AND SWING AGAINST LOD
5	SS	LF fwd in CBMP facing wall, slight turn to L; RF to side and slightly back, backing DC against LOD.
6	SS	LF back in CBMP PO DC against LOD; RF closes to LF facing DW turning lady to PP, lady faces DC.
7	SS	LF to side along LOD in PP, loosen hold slightly; swing RF fwd and across along LOD to low aerial position.
8	SS	Turning inwards to face wall and partner, RF to side against LOD in contra PP; swing LF fwd and across against LOD to low aerial position.

		CHECKED CHASSÉ TO L - R AND L SWAYS - CHECKED CHASSÉ TO R - L AND R SWAYS
9	QQS	Turning inwards to face DW and partner, LF to side along LOD, Ballroom Hold; RF closes to LF; LF to side along LOD, relax knee sltly and check, feet apart.
10	SS	Transfer weight to RF and sway to R; transfer weight to LF and sway to L, face DW.

| | QQS | Extend RF to side against LOD; LF closes to RF, face DW and partner; RF to side against LOD, relax knees slightly and check, feet apart. |
| 12 | SS | Transfer weight to LF and sway to L; transfer weight to RF and sway to R. |

Bars 9-12 are danced facing DW moving along or against LOD.

FWD LOCK STEP - 1,2,3 NATURAL TURN - NATURAL SPIN TURN AND CHECK

13	QQS	Extend LF diag fwd DW; RF crosses behind LF; LF diag fwd facing DW.
14	SQQ	RF fwd in CBMP OP DW commencing to turn R; LF to side backing DC still turning; RF closes to LF backing LOD.
15	SS	LF back down LOD and pivot to R with RF held in CBMP; RF fwd towards DC continue turn to R.
16	SS	LF to side and slightly back towards centre, short step; RF back agst LOD, slight body turn L, checking step.

To make progressive: Release hold at end of bar 4, lady making a solo Four Step to next partner on her left. Bars 5 and 6. Man may move side, close, side, close along LOD (SS, SS) to next lady.

There was a young man came from Malta,
When dancing would dawdle and falter,
But when he got going
He went like a Boeing
And landed somewhere in Gibraltar.

A dashing young dancer from Harlech
Was apt to overeat with his garlic.
The girls looked askance
When he asked them to dance
Saying, "We'd rather perform with a Dalek."

CHAPTER 3

Dances with a Scottish Flavour

CAMERON FLING

Time 2/4 or 6/8. Tempo 48.
There are many suitable tunes on Jimmy Shand's records.
Commence man and lady facing LOD, inside hands joined.
Man's steps. Lady counterpart unless otherwise stated.

Bar	Count	**FWD LOCK STEPS - OUTWARD SOLO TURN ENDING PARTNERS SQUARE**
1	1&2	LF diag fwd along LOD; RF crosses very slightly behind LF; LF diag fwd along LOD. Skipping action.
2	1&2	RF diag fwd along LOD; LF crosses very slightly behind RF; RF diag fwd along LOD. Skipping action.
3	1.2	Releasing hold, LF diag fwd towards DC commencing to turn L (lady to R); RF to side along LOD almost back to back still turning L.
4	1.2	LF to side along LOD, backing DC, still turning slightly L; RF closes to LF facing wall and partner. Adopt Double Hold.

		SIDE POINTS & CLOSES - SOLO REARWARD WALKS TO CENTRE (LADY TO WALL)
5	1.2	In Double Hold, point LF to side along LOD flinging clasped hands upwards then sideways in a curving movement; close LF to RF bringing arms to normal Double Hold pos. Head turn L on point (lady R).
6	1.2	Point RF to side against LOD flinging clasped hands upwards then sideways in a curving movement; close RF to LF bringing arms to normal Double Hold position. Head turn against LOD on point.

Arm movements are the same in both bars. Note both arms are used.

| 7 | 1.2 | Releasing hold, LF back to centre (lady RF back to wall); RF back to centre. |
| 8 | 1.2 | LF back to centre; close RF to LF. Only moderate steps last 2 bars. |

FWD LOCK STEPS TO PARTNER - L HAND AND R HAND CLAPS - OWN HAND CLAPS

9	1&2	LF diag fwd towards wall and partner; RF crosses very slightly behind LF; LF diag fwd. Skipping action.
10	1&2	RF diag fwd towards wall and partner; LF crosses very slightly behind RF; RF diag fwd. Skipping action.
11	1.2	Slap lady's L palm with own L palm; slap lady's R palm with own R palm.
12	1&2	Clap own hands 3 times.

R HAND AND L HAND CLAPS - OWN HAND CLAPS - 2 BARS NAT WALTZ TURN

13	1.2	Slap lady's R palm with own R palm; slap lady's L palm with own L palm.
14	1&2	Clap own hands 3 times.
15	1&2	Taking ballroom hold, LF to side across LOD into
16	1&2	2 bars natural waltz turn (man Pas de Valse on last bar) to finish partners facing LOD taking commencing hold and position.

To make progressive: In bars 9 and 10 man moves leftwards to next partner in front, lady moving leftwards to next partner behind.

A dashing young man from Albania
Got hooked on a jitterbug mania
But things got so hectic,
His both feet turned septic,
Said his girlfriend, "I'm sure they must pain yer."

Remember, however, that a dance a day keeps the doctor away!

SKIRL OF THE PIPES

Time 2/4 (may also be danced in 6/8). Tempo 50.
Music: Any lively Scottish tunes in sequence.
Man's steps. Lady counterpart unless otherwise st
Commence in Open Hold, partners facing along L(

Bar	Count	**LOOSE LOCKS - STEPS, SWINGS**
1	1&2	LF diag fwd along LOD; lock RF loosely behind LF; extend LF diag fwd along LOD.
2	1&2	RF diag fwd along LOD; lock LF loosely behind RF; extend RF diag fwd along LOD.
3	1.2	LF diag fwd along LOD; swing RF fwd to low aerial crossing loosely in front of LF.
4	1.2	RF diag fwd along LOD; swing LF fwd to low aerial crossing loosely in front of RF.
		FWD WALKS, CLOSE - TURN, CLOSE AND CLAP OWN HANDS - FWD, CLOSE AND CLAP OWN HANDS
5	1.2	LF fwd along LOD; RF fwd along LOD.
6	1.2	LF fwd along LOD; close RF to LF.
7	1.2	Side LF to centre; release hold and swivel inward to R (lady to L); close RF to LF without weight clapping own hands, partners facing each other, man facing wall.
8	1.2	RF fwd to wall (lady LF fwd); close LF to RF without weight clapping own hands. Take Double Hold, man still facing wall and partner.
		CHASSÉ TO L AND DOUBLE TAPS - CHASSÉ TO R AND DOUBLE TAPS
9	1.2	Side LF along LOD; close RF to LF.
10	1&2	Side LF along LOD; tap (or stamp RF twice on spot (&S). Raise L and R clasped hands.
11	1.2	Side RF against LOD; close LF to RF.
12	1&2	Side RF against LOD; tap (or stamp) LF twice on spot (&S), raising R and L clasped hands.
		STEP & SWING ALONG LOD - STEP & SWING AGAINST LOD - CHECK & TURN TO LOD
13	1.2	LF to side along LOD still Double Hold, strong step relaxing knee; swing RF fwd and across along LOD to low aerial.

Correcting swing, RF to side against LOD, strong step relaxing knee; swing LF fwd and across against LOD to low aerial.

	1.2	With LF still in aerial position, LF fwd and across against LOD in contra hold, relax knee (check); transfer weight back to RF turning inward to L (lady to R).
16	1.2	LF to side along LOD, Double Hold in PP; close RF to LF facing along LOD and releasing front hands to commencing position and hold.

To make progressive: Man releases hold and moves fwd in bars 5/6 to partner in front. Lady remains in place in bars 5/6 but closes RF to LF awaiting partner from behind.

THE TARTAN TWINKLE

Time 2/4. Tempo 48/52. Music in 6/8 time could be used but 2/4 is better with tunes like 'Scotland the Brave'.
Man's steps. Lady counterpart unless otherwise stated. Commence partners facing along LOD, inside hands joined in Open Hold.

Bar	Count	FWD WALKS - SKIPPING MOVEMENTS
1	1.2	LF fwd along LOD, inside hands joined; RF fwd along LOD.
2	1.2	LF fwd along LOD; RF fwd along LOD.
3	1&2	LF diag fwd along LOD; RF part closes towards LF; extend LF fwd along LOD.
4	1&2	RF diag fwd along LOD; LF part closes toward RF; extend RF fwd along LOD.

Skipping action on bars 3 and 4.

		STEP, POINTS ON LF & RF - TWINKLE, CLOSE
5	1.2	LF fwd along LOD, slight turn L (lady slight turn R); point RF diag fwd along LOD.
6	1.2	RF diag fwd along LOD, slight turn R to face LOD (lady slight turn L); point LF fwd along LOD, short step.
7	1.2	LF fwd along LOD, inside hands still joined; RF closes to LF.
8	1.2	LF back against LOD; RF closes back to LF, end facing slightly DC.

SOLO WALKS DC - SWIVEL HAND CLAPS - SOLO WALKS TO PARTNER AND DOUBLE STAMP

9	1.2	LF fwd towards DC releasing hold (lady moving DW); RF fwd towards DC.
10	1&2	LF fwd towards DC and swivel to L to face wall and partner (lady swivel R), RF held sltly fwd (1); clap own hands twice to the timing of '&2' and shout "Och Aye".
11	1.2	RF fwd towards centre and partner (lady LF fwd); LF fwd to centre.
12	1&2	RF fwd towards wall and partner joining hands in Double Hold (1); stamp LF twice at side of RF to the timing of '&2', (shout "the Noo" at the same time).

PAS DE BASQUE TO L AND R - FOUR STEP TO END IN COMMENCING POSITION

13	1&2	Pas de Basque to side along LOD, LF, RF, LF, Double Hold.
14	1&2	Pas de Basque to side against LOD, RF, LF,RF.
15	1.2	Still in Double Hold, LF fwd in CBMP towards wall turning to L; RF to side and slightly back, backing DC against LOD.
16	1.2	LF back under body, backing DC against LOD (lady RF fwd OP turning to R); RF closes to LF releasing lady's R hand to end in commencing position and hold.

To make progressive: Man veers to L in bars 11/12 to next partner in front; lady will veer to L to next partner behind sharing the progression. **Alternative progression:** Lady remains in place for bars 1/2 awaiting next partner from behind, man releasing hold dancing the normal 4 walks. Both progressions could be used in the same sequence.

What are the meanings of the term MC?

1.   A person who pretends to have a good knowledge of dancing.

2.   A mental case.

61

TARTAN PARADE

Time 6/8 or 2/4. Tempo around 50. Music: Happy Hours with Jimmy Shand, side 2, tracks 1 and 3, 'Music for Pleasure', MFP 4157511. Man's steps. Lady normal opposite unless otherwise stated. Commence in Double Hold, man facing wall, lady backing wall.

Bar	Count	PAS DE BASQUE TO L - PAS DE BASQUE TO R - FOUR STEP
1	1&2	Pas de Basque to L along LOD in Double Hold, LRL.
2	1&2	Pas de Basque to R against LOD, RLR.
3	1.2	LF fwd to wall turning to L; RF to side against LOD backing DC against LOD.
4	1.2	LF back DC against LOD PO on R side; close RF to LF almost facing LOD (lady turning to R OP closes LF to RF almost facing LOD). Release lady's R hand leaving inside hands joined in Open Hold.

		WALKS AND HOP ON LF - WALKS AND HOP ON RF
5	1.2	In Open Hold LF fwd along LOD (lady RF fwd); RF fwd along LOD.
6	1.2	LF fwd along LOD; hop on LF raising RF from floor, knee bent, toe pointing downward.
7	1.2	RF fwd along LOD; LF fwd along LOD.
8	1.2	RF fwd along LOD; hop on RF raising LF from the floor, knee bent, toe pointing downward.

		SIDE CLOSES TO INWARD TURN - PAS DE BASQUE L - PAS DE BASQUE R
9	1.2	LF to side towards centre turning slightly R, hold released (lady RF to side to wall turning slightly L).
10	1.2	Side and back LF towards centre turning slightly R to face wall and partner.
11	1&2	Placing L hand on hip, Pas de Basque to L along LOD, LRL raising R arm loosely above head, elbow slightly bent.
12	1&2	Placing R hand on hip, Pas de Basque to R against LOD, RLR, raising L arm loosely above head, elbow slightly bent.

SKIPPING STEPS TOWARDS PARTNER - L AND R HAND CLAPS - OWN HAND CLAPS

13	1&2	Folding arms, elbows fwd, LF fwd towards wall and partner (lady RF fwd towards centre and partner) lowering L shoulder slightly; move RF towards LF, very short step; extend LF fwd, skipping action.
14	1&2	RF fwd towards wall and partner lowering R shoulder slightly; move LF fwd towards RF, very short step; extend RF fwd, skipping action.
15	1.2	Unfold arms and slap lady's L hand with own L hand at shoulder height, LF closing to RF without weight; clap lady's R hand with own R hand.
16	1.2	Clap own hands together at shoulder height; repeat clap.

Take Double Hold at start of next sequence.

To make progressive: Man moves fwd DC in bars 9 and 10, LF, RF, LF swivelling R to face wall and next partner in front then closes RF to LF. Lady dances normal alignment.

His tango was delightful,
His waltzing was a dream,
His quickstep couldn't be bettered,
His foxtrot had to be seen.

But he couldn't guide a partner
And that's the sorry tale.
He was only a solo dancer
And a very frustrated male.

He discovered the 'slosh' and graduated to line dancing. With his Stetson, cowboy boots and bandana he is now going great guns.

KILTIE SWAY

Time 2/4 (or 6/8). Tempo 48/50. Music: Jimmy Shand, 'Music for Pleasure', MFP 4157511, side 2, track 1 (6/8) and track 3 (2/4) or any Gay Gordons medley.
Man's steps. Lady counterpart unless otherwise stated.
Commence in Double Hold, man facing wall and partner.

Bar	Count	**PAS DE BASQUE TO L - PAS DE BASQUE TO R - SIDE STEPS AND CLOSES ALONG LOD**
1	1&2	Pas de Basque to L along LOD; LRL.
2	1&2	Pas de Basque to R against LOD, RLR.
3	1.2	LF to side along LOD; close RF to LF.
4	1.2	LF to side along LOD; close RF to LF.

		PAS DE BASQUE TO L - PAS DE BASQUE TO R - PROMENADE WALKS
5	1&2	Pas de Basque along LOD, LRL.
6	1&2	Pas de Basque to R against LOD, RLR.
7	1.2	LF to side along LOD turning outward to PP still in Double Hold; RF fwd and across along LOD.
8	1.2	LF to side along LOD; close RF to LF in PP.

		STEPS AND TAPS - TURNING TWINKLE - STEP, CLOSE TO PARTNER
9	1.2	LF to side along LOD releasing front hands turning slightly L (lady turn R); tap RF near to LF, face DC (lady face DW).
10	1.2	RF diag fwd along LOD turning slightly R (lady tn L); tap LF at side of RF, face DW (lady face DC).
11	1.2	LF to side twds centre releasing hold and tng R (lady turn L on RF); close RF to LF facing wall and partner.
12	1.2	LF fwd to wall and partner (lady RF fwd to centre and partner); close RF to LF, partners normal distance apart. Do not take hold.

		SLAP L HAND PALMS - SLAP R HAND PALMS - CLAP OWN HANDS - L AND R SWAYS
13	1.2	Slap palm of L hand against palm of lady's L hand at about shoulder height, man's hand moving further than lady's hand; repeat palm slaps using R hands.

14	1&2	Clap own hands 3 times at chest height preparing to take Double Hold.
15	1.2	Rejoin both hands and with knees relaxed, feet in place, sway to L from waist; sway to R from waist.
16	1.2	Repeat sways as bar 15 to end in commencing position (bars 15 and 16 may be expressed freely).

To make progressive: Man release hold at end of bar 6 and dances solo for bars 7 and 8 to next partner in front. Lady remains in place bars 7 and 8 awaiting next partner from behind.

WHITE HEATHER PARADE

Time 2/4 or 6/8. Tempo 48/50.
Man's steps given. Lady's steps normal opposite.
Commence partners facing LOD, inside hands joined in Open Hold.

Bar	Count	FWD LOCK STEPS - 4 WALKS
1	1&2	LF diag fwd along LOD (lady RF); cross RF loosely behind LF; LF diag fwd along LOD.
2	1&2	RF diag fwd along LOD; cross LF loosely behind RF; RF diag fwd along LOD.
3	1.2	LF fwd along LOD; RF fwd along LOD.
4	1.2	LF fwd along LOD; RF fwd along LOD.
		FWD LOCK STEPS - STEP AND SWING - SIDE AND CLOSE
5	1&2	LF diag fwd along LOD; cross RF loosely behind RF; LF diag fwd along LOD.
6	1&2	RF diag fwd along LOD; cross LF loosely behind RF; RF diag fwd along LOD.
7	1.2	LF diag fwd along LOD taking lady's R hand in Double Hold in PP, slight stamp action; swing RF fwd and across along LOD to low aerial.
8	1.2	Turning to R, RF to side against LOD; close LF to RF without weight facing wall and partner still in Double Hold.

PAS DE BASQUE TO L AND R - L AND R HAND CLAPS - OWN HAND CLAPS

9	1&2	Pas de Basque to L along LOD, LRL.
10	1&2	Pas de Basque to R against LOD, RLR, then release hold keeping hands at shoulder level.
11	1.2	Clap own L hand with lady's L hand, do not hold; repeat clapping using R hand to R hand.
12	1&2	Clap own hands 3 times still facing wall and partner.

SIDE CLOSES - PAS DE BASQUE TO L AND R

13	1.2	Taking lady's R hand in own L hand and placing R hand on hip - LF to side along LOD, headlines against LOD; close RF to LF.
14	1.2	Repeat bar 13 - side, close, face wall and partner.
15	1&2	Pas de Basque to L along LOD, LRL, man's R hand still on R hip.
16	1&2	Pas de Basque to R against LOD, RLR, releasing hold and turning slightly to L (lady to R) to end in commencing position and taking lady's L hand in own R hand during the bar.

To make progressive: Lady remains stationary in bars 3 and 4 (walks) awaiting next partner from behind. Man makes normal movement in bars 3 and 4 (4 walks) to next partner in front and joins hands.

Alternatively, lady may make progression, man remaining in place.

This man went to a Fancy Dress Dance the other night with his girl but he only had one ticket. He gave his partner a 'piggy back', covered her with a top coat and went as a tortoise. The suspicious doorkeeper asked what was on his back. He replied, "It's Michelle."

THE PIPER'S PARADE

Time 2/4 or 6/8. Tempo 48/50.
Music: Any Gay Gordons medleys.
Man's steps. Lady counterpart unless otherwise stated.
Commence partners facing LOD, inside hands joined in Open Hold.

Bar	Count	**FORWARD WALKS - HEEL AND TOE POINTS AND REPEAT**
1	1.2	LF fwd along LOD; RF fwd along LOD.
2	1.2	LF fwd along LOD; close RF to LF, still face LOD.
3	1.2	Keeping weight on RF, LF diag fwd, face LOD (heel); move LF back to RF, knee relaxed, point toe to floor crossing loosely in front of RF.
4	1.2	Repeat bar 3, heel and toe points (free arms may be held aloft in bars 3 and 4).

FWD LOCKS - FWD WALKS (LADY ALLEMANDE)

5	1&2	LF fwd along LOD in Open Hold; cross RF loosely behind LF; extend LF fwd along LOD.
6	1&2	RF fwd along LOD; LF crosses loosely behind RF; extend RF along LOD. Partners move slightly inwards towards each other in this bar taking Double Hold in PP, man facing DW, lady facing DC.
7	1.2	LF to side along LOD releasing lady's L hand as she commences to turn R under man's raised L arm; RF fwd and across along LOD (lady LF to side and back, backing LOD still turning R).
8	1.2	LF to side along LOD taking lady's R hand in Double Hold (lady RF to side along LOD having completed tn to R); close RF to LF, man face DW, lady face DC.

STEP AND SWING - STEP BACK AND DOUBLE STAMPS - REPEAT

9	1.2	LF to side along LOD still in Double Hold in PP; swing RF fwd and across along LOD to low aerial.
10	1&2	RF back against LOD; stamp LF at side of RF (&); repeat stamp (2).

| 11 | 1.2 | LF to side along LOD; swing RF fwd and across along LOD to low aerial. |
| 12 | 1&2 | RF back against LOD; stamp LF at side of RF (&); repeat stamp (2); (check). |

REARWARD WALKS - FWD OPEN CHASSÉS (SKIPPING MOVEMENTS)

13	1.2	LF back against LOD releasing lady's R hand, inside hands only joined; RF back against LOD in Open Hold.
14	1.2	LF back against LOD; close RF back to LF, partners facing LOD in commencing hold and position.
15	1&2	LF fwd along LOD; half close RF towards LF; extend LF fwd along LOD (skipping movement). Move slightly DC in this bar (lady slightly DW).
16	1&2	RF fwd along LOD; half close LF towards RF; extend RF fwd along LOD (skipping movement). Move slightly DW in this bar (lady slightly DC).

To make progressive: Man releases hold at end of bar 14 and dances chassés solo to next partner in front. Lady remains in place during bars 15 and 16 awaiting next partner from behind.

SCOTTISH SWING

Time 6/8 (or 2/4). Tempo 54/56.
Partners commence facing LOD in Open Hold.
Man's steps. Lady's contra unless stated otherwise.

Bar Count
1	1.2	LF fwd along LOD, inside hands joined; RF fwd along LOD, commence to turn R (lady to L).
2	1.2	LF to side along LOD releasing hands still turning R and taking lady's R hand in own L hand; cross RF behind LF, partners now backing LOD and preparing to twist.
3	1.2	On ball of LF and heel of RF twist to R (lady to L)
4	1.2	releasing hold, end facing LOD weight on RF and join inside hands. The twist takes 2 bars (or count 4 beats).

5	1.2	LF to side towards centre, small step; swing RF diag across LF to low aerial position (lady RF to side, swing LF across).
6	1.2	RF to side towards wall and partner, short step; swing LF diag across RF.
7	1.2	Correcting swing LF fwd along LOD; RF fwd along LOD turning to R (lady to L).
8	1.2	LF to side along LOD facing wall and partner, hold released, still turning R and taking lady's R hand in own L hand; hop on LF, partners facing against LOD, R knee bent, R toe pointing downwards.
9	1.2	Repeat movement of bars 7 and 8 against LOD
10	1.2	commencing on RF, turning L and hopping on RF. End partners facing LOD, join inside hands.
11-12	---	Repeat bars 7 and 8, step and swings.
13	1.2	LF to side towards centre (lady RF towards wall) releasing hold; cross RF over LF moving twds centre, placing R hand on hip and raising L hand above head.
14	1&2	LF to side towards centre turning R to face wall and partner; tap or stamp RF twice to floor at side of LF (count '&2').
15	1.2	RF fwd towards wall and partner; LF fwd placing L hand on hip and raising R hand above head, commence to turn L (lady to R).
16	1&2	RF to side facing LOD joining inside hands; tap or stamp LF twice to floor at side of RF (count '&2'). Rejoin inside hands.

To make progressive: Man veers slightly L in bars 15 and 16 to next partner in front. Lady veers slightly L to next partner behind.

> *He thought he was good in a swing*
> *As he danced with a pretty young thing*
> *But her feet got so sore*
> *She could stand it no more*
> *And retired with her feet in a sling.*

SCOTLAND THE BRAVE

Time 2/4. Tempo around 50.
Music: 'Scotland the Brave' or any lively Scottish tune.
Man's steps. Lady counterpart unless otherwise stated. Commence partners facing along LOD, inside hands joined in Open Hold.

Bar	Count	SKIPPING MOVEMENTS - FWD WALKS AND CLOSE
1	1&2	LF fwd along LOD slightly DC (lady DW); RF part closes to LF; extend LF fwd.
2	1&2	RF fwd along LOD slightly DW (lady DC); LF part closes to RF; extend RF fwd.

Dance bars 1 and 2 with a skipping action.

3	1.2	LF fwd along LOD; RF fwd along LOD.
4	1.2	LF fwd along LOD; RF closes to LF.

Last 2 bars danced in jaunty manner.

		POINT DC AND CLOSE - POINT DW AND CLOSE - REARWARD WALKS AND CLOSE
5	1.2	Point LF diag fwd DC (lady point RF DW), relax R knee slightly; close LF to RF with weight.
6	1.2	Point RF diag fwd DW (lady point LF DC), relax L knee slightly; close RF to LF with weight, preparing to move rearward.
7	1.2	LF back against LOD; LF back against LOD.
8	1.2	LF back against LOD; RF closes to LF.

Last 2 bars danced in jaunty manner.

		OUTWARD TURN, POINT & CLAP OWN HANDS - INWARD TURN, POINT & CLAP OWN HANDS
9	1.2	Releasing hold - LF fwd along LOD, slight turn L to face DC (lady turns R on RF to face DW); point RF to side and fwd, short step, clapping own hands at the same time.
10	1.2	RF diag fwd turning inward to R (lady to L); point LF to side and fwd, short step clapping own hands at the same time, face DW (lady face DC).
11	1.2	Repeat the turn, point and clap movements of bars 9/10.
12	1.2	Repeat turn, point and clap movement of bar 11. Join hands in PP, Double Hold, man fcg DW, lady fcg DC.

FWD & REARWARD WALKS TO INWARD TN - PAS DE BASQUE TO L - PAS GLISSÉ TO R

13	1.2	LF to side along LOD in PP, Double Hold; RF fwd and across along LOD, relax knee (check).
14	1.2	Extend LF back against LOD turning inward to R (lady to L); RF to side against LOD facing wall and partner and brushing LF to RF.
15	1&2	LF to side along LOD into Pas de Basque, LF, RF, LF.
16	1.2	RF to side against LOD turning outward to face LOD releasing front hands; LF closes back to RF without weight to end in commencing position and hold.

To make progressive: Lady remains in place for bars 3 and 4, man dancing his normal movement to partner in front.

May be danced in 6/8 time or as a quickstep.

Remember that party dances mean what they are, so dance lightheartedly.

---

*Cynthia's dream dance was the bossa nova
But she was grabbed by the local Casanova.
When he started his tricks
He received painful kicks.
Both were glad when the bossa nova was over.*

*Dancing is never boring with the right partner.
(With the wrong partner it may still be an experience to remember.)*

When selecting a lady for a partner make sure you can find one who can move backwards without looking over her shoulder to see where she's going.

Keep fit - Keep young - Keep it up!

OBSERVATIONS ON THE MSD BIRD

As a musician and a naturalist I have recently noticed an increase in the number of Modern Sequence Dancing Birds. These are much like the domestic species but show a greater sureness of movement, better powers of observation and a thinly-veiled joy in actually being alive. These birds can be seen in all their glory at their meetings held in school halls, community centres, licensed premises and ballrooms where they indulge the activity from which they take their name Modern Sequence Dancing.

The size of the meeting place is not important as the flock expands (by Parkinson's law) to fill the space available. A good floor is desirable but far more important is that there must be a perch for each bird present - no bird would tolerate not having a perch. Although the casual observer may wonder at this since more time is spent dancing than perching - nevertheless it is one of the prime rules of the species

This same observer may also assume that any bird may perch anywhere but it will be seen that each bird perches in the same place each week and will resist strongly any attempt at encroachment on its territory. Observe the experienced stranger who first visits one of the colonies and he will be seen to carry out the following curious routine. He will present himself for admission some 10 or 15 minutes after the advertised time of commencement. Should a dance be in progress, on entering the hall he will stand and admire the decor, read a notice on the wall, tie his shoelace or visit the toilet, until the dance has ended. When all the dancers are settled he will then take up a perch furthest away from the rest. He will ON NO ACCOUNT remove from a perch any scarf, shoe, handbag, cardigan or such, for by that sign all will know that the perch is reserved for an absent member. (A count at one meeting revealed that when the dance began, although there were only 15 members present, 47 perches were reserved.)

Now to the dances themselves. These are governed by an Emsee who tells the rest of the flock which dance to do next and, with his mate, shows them how. Having got most of the flock on the floor he will often leave his mate and take up one of the hen-birds who may be on her perch. When the dance ends, all the flock retire to their perches except Emsee who looks in a book to see how to do the next dance.

Dances, although differing from each other, have one thing in common - they must be performed in a laid-down sequence and all pairs do the same part of that sequence at the same time. To make sure no-one is in doubt, Emsee moves amongst his flock uttering shrill cries such as "Whisk", "Feather", "Twinkle", "Telemark", "Spin" or "Fishtail" which, although so much gibberish to the untutored, serves to bring his flock into line and adds to his (Emsee's) prestige. Individualism is strictly forbidden - offenders are quickly put in their place by Emsee and persistent non-conformists escorted to their perches. There they sit for a while with ruffled plumage until, finally, ostracised by the rest of the flock, they withdraw.

But whilst the MSD Bird is remorseless towards those who refuse to toe the 'party line', it is just as ready to help those who show the least inclination to 'have a go'. An urge seems to fill every breast to impart knowledge to the ignorant and many a seasoned member can be seen explaining to the untutored a particular step, presumably to convince them that Emsee's ejaculation of "Fish-tail", etc. was not meant as an expression of opinion or personal abuse.

Dances are usually performed to recorded music although musicians are sometimes employed. Canned music is cheaper and the timing can be adjusted by Emsee to suit the needs of the dancers who would otherwise complain. Musicians tend to be despised by dancers because they lack the knowledge of the sequences and yet sometimes they are welcomed since both flock and Emsee can then unite in their complaints regarding tempo, volume, etc.

This tendency to complain seems to be inherent in the species. In the same evening the following remarks can be heard:- "It's stuffy in here tonight", "It's draughty in here tonight", "They're not very stylish dancers", "I wish they wouldn't pose so much", "This floor's too

73

slippery", "There's a sticky patch down by the band", "This music is too fast", "... too slow", "... too loud", "... no beat", etc., etc., etc.

New sequence dances are collected with the same enthusiasm that Red Indians collected scalps and usually for the same reason - so they can show their less adventurous or less capable comrades their prowess. Some members of a flock travel vast distances to learn a new routine and, on return to the home meeting, will use every known art and device to persuade Emsee to allow them to demonstrate this dance. By so doing they will earn the admiration, envy or derision of the rest of the flock depending upon whether the demonstrators are popular, whether there is a sincere desire to pass on the new dance or whether they are just being 'cocky with it'. Fortunately Emsee can usually keep one jump ahead by using a mysterious document called a 'script' which, bristling with 'PP', 'CBMP', 'LOD', 'ww' and the like, is nearly as easy to decipher by the rank and file as the Dead Sea Scrolls.

To summarise the characteristics of the MSD Bird as intolerant, demanding, inconsistent, extrovert and quick to take offence (traits not unknown even in human species) would be less than fair. Unlike most dancing types they really enjoy their dances because of the dancing and not as an excuse for late drinking like most Modern Dancing Birds. Not only do they enjoy dancing for its own sake but they can be seen to enjoy it - if one looks beyond the frowns and grimaces thrown at the band. Furthermore they have the most generous hearts in the world and no worthy cause - whether national, parochial or individual - can complain of the support given by them. Finally, they revel in the spirit engendered by fancy dress and join with gusto into any such function, as they can and do (I hope!) enjoy a laugh at themselves.

A MUSICIAN

(Updated from a feature written by the musician Phil Swetman in the 1960's.)